Samuel Wilberforce

The Victor in the conflict

sermons preached during the season of Lent

Samuel Wilberforce

The Victor in the conflict
sermons preached during the season of Lent

ISBN/EAN: 9783744745017

Printed in Europe, USA, Canada, Australia, Japan

Cover: Foto ©Lupo / pixelio.de

More available books at **www.hansebooks.com**

The Victor in the Conflict.

SERMONS

PREACHED DURING

THE SEASON OF LENT, 1867,

IN

OXFORD.

BY

THE LORD BISHOP OF OXFORD.
REV. H. P. LIDDON, M.A.
THE DEAN OF CORK.
REV. CANON WOODFORD.
REV. DR. PUSEY.
THE LORD BISHOP OF MEATH.

REV. M. F. SADLER, M.A.
REV. DR. KAY.
REV. T. T. CARTER, M.A.
REV. G. BULSTRODE, M.A.
REV. R. RANDALL, M.A.
ARCHDEACON BICKERSTETH.

WITH A PREFACE

BY

SAMUEL, LORD BISHOP OF OXFORD.

Oxford,
AND 377, STRAND, LONDON:
JAMES PARKER AND CO.
1868.

PREFACE.

THE Sermons preached at St. Mary's and St. Giles' Churches in Oxford, on the Wednesdays and Fridays in Lent, 1867, concluded a series which had lasted through some preceding years. The strife between good and evil had been followed out, so far as revelation supplied matter for the enquiry, from this world to the world of spirits. It remained to examine the records of its close, and to exhibit to the eyes of the faithful the Victor in that long conflict. It was this which was attempted in the series of 1867.

In 1868, the subject which had been suggested in the former course, and without which it was incomplete, and yet which could not then be followed without unduly disturbing the sequence of those Sermons,—the responsibility of man as a creature to his Creator,—with the ideas which flow directly from it, was taken as the leading subject of the course. No former course appeared to create and maintain to the end such a living interest amidst the large congregations which filled both churches.

May God grant, by His great grace, that some enduring results to the furtherance of His glory, and the benefit of His holy Church, may flow from the preaching and publication of these Sermons.

S. OXON.

CUDDESDON PALACE,
Sept. 21, 1868.

CONTENTS.

SERMON I.
(p. 1.)
The Victor, in the Counsels of Eternity.
REVELATIONS xiii. 8.
BY THE LORD BISHOP OF OXFORD.

SERMON II.
(p. 13.)
The Victor, in the Times of Preparation.
ISAIAH xl. 3.
BY H. P. LIDDON, M.A.

SERMON III.
(p. 35.)
The Victor, manifest in the Flesh.
ROMANS viii. 2.
BY THE DEAN OF CORK.

SERMON IV.
(p. 59.)
The Victor, exalted to His Throne.
DANIEL vii. 13.
BY J. R. WOODFORD, M.A.

SERMON V.
(p. 73.)
The Victor, on His Throne, the Object of Divine Worship.
REVELATIONS v. 11—13.
BY E. B. PUSEY, D.D.

SERMON VI.
(p. 99.)
The Victor, on His Throne, the Mediator between God and Man.
HEBREWS vii. 25.
BY THE LORD BISHOP OF MEATH.

SERMON VII.
(p. 115.)
The Victor, on His Throne, the Priest of His People.
HEBREWS vii. 26.
BY M. F. SADLER, M.A.

SERMON VIII.
(p. 133.)
The Victor, on His Throne, giving Gifts to Men.
EPHESIANS iv. 7—12.
BY W. KAY, D.D.

SERMON IX.
(p. 145.)
The Victor, on His Throne, mystically United to His People.
ST. JOHN xvii. 10.
BY T. T. CARTER, M.A.

SERMON X.

(p. 161.)

The Victor, on His Throne, absolving His People.

St. Matthew vii. 29 ; St. John xx. 23.

By G. BULSTRODE, M.A.

SERMON XI.

(p. 185.)

The Victor, on His Throne, holding the Keys of Hell and of Death.

Acts vii. 59.

By R. RANDALL, M.A.

SERMON XII.

(p. 201.)

The Victor, on His Throne, delivering up the Kingdom.

1 Cor. xv. 28.

By ARCHDEACON BICKERSTETH.

ERRATUM.

p. 142, line 12, *for* Wilfred *read* Winfred.

SERMON I.

The Victor, in the Counsels of Eternity.

REVELATIONS xiii. 8.
"The Lamb slain from the foundation of the world."

"THE Victor in the Counsels of Eternity." What words, brethren, for us to utter! What thoughts for us to muse upon! We—creatures of a day—creatures not merely under the narrow circumscribing law of time, which at its widest expansion and longest duration is but a poor finite measure, incapable of shewing even as a point beside eternity; but yet more,—under that law of time in its most cramping measures: creatures to whom time is dropped out by minutes; who are born but to die; whose longest life is "even as a vapour, which appeareth for a little while, and then vanisheth away,"—we can scarcely speak about the counsels of eternity. Our speculating on them at all is as if a creature, which by the law of its being was chained to some living stalk, which had fixed itself in the narrow chink of some riven rock whence it floated idly in the lazy current of the half-stagnant tide, should speculate upon the mighty currents of the neighbouring ocean, as it surged by in its deep azure mystery. And even this is an unworthy and incompetent analogy. For nearer far in relative magnitude is the least of these half-animated zoophytes to the mighty ocean with all its trackless unmeasured depths, than is one drop of Time to the illimitable sea of Eternity.

For what is eternity? how can our minds even grasp the very idea of what is so unlike anything around us in this world, which is bound so fast beneath the bonds of time and space, of extension and succession. For eternity is not time prolonged; no, not to the uttermost prolongation through which, by heaping in thought millions upon millions, we strain the weary imagination to get something like a calculation of its infinity. It is not this at all; it is not time prolonged, but time abolished; it is not the lengthening out of the narrow stream as it toils on between the banks, broken into many a reach, marked out by many a boundary, losing the past and hiding the future by many a winding; it is not this: it is the boundless, shoreless, indivisible unity of the measureless ocean, where past is not, nor future, nor fading, nor darkness, but the all ever-present now. THE COUNSELS OF ETERNITY! They reach us as the echo on the shore when the mighty storm breaks in its thunder upon the tossed-up billows of the far-off ocean-tide. They come from the trackless distances which lie beyond space itself, and seem too great for thought.

But, further, between Whom are these counsels taken? Who are those who framed them? Who are these "inhabiters of eternity?" Between the Three Divine Persons in the ever-blessed Godhead; These are the counsels of the unsearchable Trinity; of the Father, and the Son, and the Holy Ghost. The counsels of Love, of Wisdom, of Power, which are not qualities, but essences; the counsels of the Father, the fountain of Godhead; the counsels of the Son, begotten before all worlds, one in the unbroken unity of the Godhead, co-equal, co-eternal with the Father, but from the Father, as the Father is not from Him; Who is the Father's Word, the coming forth to all created being of the Father's glory; the counsels of the Holy Ghost, one God with the Father and with the Son; from the Father and from the Son, the Lord of love, of light, of life; Their counsels; Their "Let *us* make man;" Their secret, trackless, thought-transcending plans! Surely, as we gaze reverently, through the mist which hangs over eternity, at the council-chamber of the mysterious Three in One, we feel that the majesty of the words we utter, even transcends our thoughts, and we might turn away heart-struck from these counsels of eternity. Yet this passage declares to us most plainly their existence: "The Lamb slain from the foundation of the world." The question which undoubtedly exists, whether in the true construction that "from the foundation of the world" belongs directly to "the Lamb slain," or to "the Lamb's book of life," makes no difference here. Either interpretation equally presupposes the counsel in that awful council chamber; the pre-ordaining plan; the predetermined end. Nor does the passage stand alone. Listen to the words of Zechariah: "Awake, O sword, against My Shepherd, and against the Man that is My fellow, saith the Lord of Hosts[a]." How are the stirrings of His hidden will Who is "the mighty God, great in counsel, mighty in work[b]," set before us in this grand chant of ancient prophecy! How do we hear Him "declaring the end from the beginning, and from ancient times the things that are not yet done, saying, My counsel shall stand, and I will do all My pleasure[c]." For all this is indeed but the ushering into Time from the circumambient Eternity of Him who is "the Ruler

[a] Zech. xiii. 7. [b] Jer. xxxii. 18, 19. [c] Isa. xlvi. 10.

in Israel, whose goings forth have been from of old, from everlasting [d]."

It is, then, plainly revealed to us that there were these counsels of eternity. And this year we propose to follow up, even into them, the subject which now for the last two seasons has occupied these our Lenten lectures. We would complete these two series of sermons in which we have seen the conflict of Christ through His Church; first, with the evil which is in this world; and next, with evil as it is impersonate in the Prince of the powers of the air, and in the hosts of his vassals, by now examining His own personal conflict with it; by tracing up the strife from His to Him, from the subject to the Lord, from the visible earthly servant to Him the unseen Lord, who gave His Saint the victory, standing by Him and making Him more than conqueror. This tracing, then, of the great Victor's path must, if it is to be complete, lead us up to its very beginning; and it began here in the counsels of eternity.

Besides, moreover, the logical fitness of beginning our enquiry here, there are some most important practical considerations into which we shall be led, and for the sake of which, even if there were no other reason for doing so, it would be well to trace back the strife and the victory to this their marvellous beginning.

For, first, in such an enquiry, we shall be drawn out of that miserable subjective mode of dealing with these great truths of the Gospel which is so common in this day; and which is full of danger; having, amongst its other evils, such a tendency to develope, under the garb of high devotional feeling, a most refined spiritual selfishness. We may trace the working of this evil in the way in which the great doctrine of the atonement is often

[d] Micah v. 2.

handled. Men speak of the necessity of our Lord becoming man that He might die for us, and the necessity of His being God that an infinite value might be imparted to His sacrifice, so that He might atone for us. In a certain sense, of course both these assertions are true; He did obey and suffer as man; and as He who obeyed and suffered was the eternal Son of the Father, He did expiate as God; but there is a too common mode of so dwelling on these mysteries of the Divine love as to exalt man into the very centre of all being. All is for him. The Son of God becomes Man; nay, men almost imply that He is God because it is necessary for us that He should be. A strange perversion of the highest truth, so as to turn it into deadly error; making God to be for the sake of man, instead of seeing that man exists at all only because it pleased God that he should be; that he is but the mere breath of God's Will, which is another name for His Love. If we would be free from this wretched blinding self-exaltation, we must approach these deep contemplations from the side of God, not from the side of man.

Go, then, with me, brethren, for a few moments, into these vast truths. See all creation, every being and thing which is, IN God before it had any derived existence, FOR God when it had been made to be. See God as the cause of creation. Understand that whilst out of God there is no necessity which can limit or constrain His perfect being, His very perfection makes Him to be a law to Himself: that His Love could not be solitary and barren, but required from its own essential perfection to be prolific; to pour itself out into a creation of derived beings, who should be capable of blessedness in doing that which His Will appointed as the perfecting of their own nature. So gazing into the mystery of creation, we can in some degree understand the Divine Perfection calling into existence personal beings endowed with reason, possessed of a real will, having a true power of choice both of good and of evil; of that which His Will in its perfectness chose for them as their blessedness, or of that which was contrary to His Will, and so to their own true happiness; even though this involved the possible development of evil. For, so far as we can see, that possibility was essential to the existence of reasonable creatures, who should possess a true power of choice, and therefore a real capacity for loving Him and rejoicing in Him, by the free action of the wills which He had created. For such a capacity would seem to be essential to the existence of a real, separate, reasonable personality, since, if it were not in these creatures of His hand, they would be but repetitions of Himself, and the universe would be peopled with nothing better than the painted and fantastic rays of the Pantheist's dream. Such a creation could not have satisfied that great Love which was the motive cause of the existence of all derived being. Rather, as we have seen, the law of its own perfectness required the existence of reasonable creatures with an independent will, able, as the result of their own choice, to share the blessedness of their Creator.

And yet further, we may see not only that this coming in of sin, through the evil choice of true free agents, may probably have been a necessary condition of the creation of such beings; but that in making redemption from sin possible, it made also possible higher actings of the Divine love than mere creation could have given room for; and further still, that it provided for a blessedness in the redeemed creation, of which it would not otherwise have been capable. Therefore, it may be, it was planned in the Counsels of Eternity. For we must not deem of redemption, or of the wonder of the Incarnation by which it was wrought out, as if they were in any sense an after-thought;—the mending of a broken plan;—the supplying by a new expedient that which in the first design had failed. Far otherwise; before any derived being was, the entrance of evil into the universe, and the fall of man was foreseen; and, withal, the opportunity it afforded for the acting of a love higher than the love even of a Creator. For great as is the love which we may trace in creation, surely we can see that for Him who, for Himself, needed not any out of Himself, and who leaving the lost in their loss, by His mere Word could have called into being hosts of other creatures to fill up the places of the fallen,—for Him to stoop so low as to knit in the Divine person of the Eternal Son the fallen nature to Himself, that He who was God might, as man, obey, suffer, and die,—surely we can see in this a love more stupendous than the love which made creation to be. This, then, the love of God required, that He might satisfy that pouring-out of love which belonged to His eternal perfection. Into this shoreless ocean, swelled, in the Counsels of Eternity, the mighty tides of the foreknowing love of God.

Secondly, whilst these Counsels of Eternity thus made provision for the acting of the Divine love, they provided also for the greater blessedness of the reasonable creation.

For the truest blessedness of every reasonable creature consists in knowing God. Out of God there is to such a being weariness, wasting, and the never-ending pangs of unsatisfied desire. For only in God can one capable of comprehending God find enough to satisfy his need. And to the increase of this comprehension there can be no limit. Ever, through eternity, may the finite, even when, according to his limited nature, he is perfect, find more and more in the infinite, and yet never exhaust that infinity. Whatever, therefore, displays more thoroughly the perfection of the All-Perfect to His creatures, provides in that display for their greater blessedness. Now, even our limited moral powers can perceive that the moral greatness which finds its perfection in love is a far nobler attribute of being than mere power. So we measure such qualities in one another: so, prolonging infinitely, with humble adoration, the lines of thought, we may estimate the attributes of God. In planning, then, redemption, and the Victor's triumph over sin and evil in the Counsels of Eternity, we may see that the All-wise provided for the revelation of the wonders of His glory, and so, for the blessedness of every blessed being, even as He never could have done by a mere creation in which was not the possbility of any fall.

Nor is all this merely a speculation, however lofty, bare of direct practical results. Besides, first, helping greatly, as I have said, to free men from the narrowing influences of a mere subjective and human view of the mystery of Redemption, it may, secondly, answer many of the doubts which rise in the mind as it dwells upon the littleness of man and the awful grandeur of the doctrine of the Incarnation of the eternal Son. Who has not, at times, been tried by such? Who has looked up into the heaven above him, and noted, as in the frosty sky they sparkle over him, the innumerable stars, and, taught by science, has learned to resolve the blue light of the milky way into yet other galaxies of more distant worlds of light — who has so gazed in wonder on the endless prodigality of creation, and mused upon the problem whether all those worlds are full, like this, of reasonable beings, without the question rising on his thoughts, how it can be that the Son of God should become incarnate for the dwellers on this single globe? It is such a drop in the expanse of ocean; such a grain in the universe; such a speck in the illimitable heavens: what could have given to its inhabitants the priceless value which called down for them, and clothed in their likeness, the eternal Son of the everlasting Father? How can it be, that whilst He took not on Him the nature of angels, He should for us and for our salvation stoop to be born of the Virgin, and become man? Now the answer to this seems to lie in that view of redemption which we have reached above. Not for man only was the marvel wrought. The mighty current of the divine love needed those vast banks through which to pour itself forth, and by their sides were ranged the whole reasonable creation of God. This speck of earth is the theatre of the universe. In the Counsels of Eternity it was fore-ordained that, here on earth, the mighty Victor should accomplish His conquests, and display to every creature the unknown marvels of the love of God. Not to rouse from man's heart only the song of thanksgiving, but to heighten the joy, and exalt the praise of all the heavenly host, did God display here the wonders of redemption. Bending from their golden thrones to gaze into the depth of the humiliation of their Lord, the highest seraphs of the Presence sought, and learned to know, in man's salvation, more of God's glory. "Which things the angels desire to look into."

Thirdly, here is another most practical and momentous conclusion, from this aspect of redemption.

If it be true of the race that it was thus redeemed, not as some afterthought, but in the Counsels of Eternity, it must be as really true of every separate soul. For, to God, the foreknowledge must be not of the race but of the individuals. It is a consequence of our infirmity that we lose the separate figures in the mass. It cannot be so with the Almighty. Each soul which He creates stands before Him in its singleness as if no other existed. Each soul which, in time, He should quicken, lay in idea as clear before Him in the back eternity. This is what constitutes the priceless value of a single soul, which makes it such an utter loss if a man should gain the whole world and lose his own soul; that it was foreknown in the counsels of eternity; that over it brooded then the Love of the Almighty; that for it the eternal Son consented to die; that it the eternal Spirit waited to sanctify.

What a grandeur does it give to these lives of ours. With what an awfulness does it invest every detail of our moral and spiritual struggle. The lines of the most common life were laid in the Counsels of Eternity. See, then, thou foreknown man, what is really passing around and within thee, in the seeming commonness of thy daily life. All was ordained for thee before the foundations of the world were laid. The mystery of thy freewill, that essential condition of thy moral trial, was held for thee by the hand of the Almighty, uninterrupted, uninfringed. Thou only, for thyself, couldst cause thy everlasting loss. But all was planned for thee, planned in love and wisdom infinite, to work out thy salvation. And this extends to every minutest detail of thy life of trial. To thy God there is neither great nor little: these measuring lines of the finite reach not to the infinite. Each detail of thy life lay in calm clearness before the gaze of the all-comprehending eye. The temptations of thy daily life; the rebellion of thy appetites; the waywardness of thy temper; the restlessness of thy intellect; the doubtfulness of thy spirit; thy companions; the small incidents of every day; this Lenten Service; the words thou art now hearing; the stirring of thy spirit under them; the yearning of thy heart; thy reluctance to give up this small passing, perishing pleasure—all were seen; as to each the love of God ordered all that was needed for thy salvation. This is thy life: fleeting as it is, it rises out of this abyss of the Divine Will, it shall be prolonged into the mysterious vistas of the coming eternity. Its lines were laid before the world was; its being shall endure when the world has passed away.

Dare, then, to look calmly, deeply, into it. Be real. See how entirely real is everything around thee. Thou hast passed, for this thy life's span, out of the darkness in which God had hid from eternity thy life, into the light and sunshine, and now under His eye thou hast to do thy part. Beside thee stands the mighty loving Victor in the Counsels of Eternity; in thee, by thee, with thee, He would conquer. Wilt thou dishonour Him? The salvation of thy soul shall be His glory. O, then, be real; real in struggling with thy common temptations; real in thy prayers; real in the self-denials, and self-watchings of this Lent; real in thy reaching after Him; real in thy finding Him in His Word; in meditation; above all, in the communion given thee of His Body and His Blood; and in this conflict He will never forget, never leave thee, and in the hour of death He shall reveal Himself to thy astonished soul, as having been even in thy passing life the mighty Victor in the Counsels of Eternity.

SERMON II.

The Victor, in the Times of Preparation.

ISAIAH xl. 3.

"The voice of him that crieth in the wilderness, Prepare ye the way of the Lord; make straight in the desert a highway for our God."

ALL the four Evangelists refer these words to the ministry of St. John the Baptist; in St. John they received their highest and complete fulfilment. But their first and historical reference is to the return of the Jewish captives from Babylon. The Lord was the King of the chosen people; and in the vision of the Prophet the promised return to home and freedom was to be a triumphant procession across the desert, headed by Israel's invisible Monarch. The cause of the holy people was the cause of God; their bondage and shame in Babylon, although a heaven-sent punishment, had been a humiliation for the majesty of Jehovah before the face of the scoffing heathen; their triumphant return would be the work of God, it would also be the manifestation of His glory. No obstacle should stop the path of His resistless advance: "Every valley shall be exalted, and every mountain and hill shall be made low: and the crooked shall be made straight, and the rough places plain: and the glory of the Lord shall be revealed, and all flesh shall see it together: for the mouth of the Lord hath spoken it."

Clearly, my brethren, there is here a wider reach of meaning than any which can be satisfied by the actual prospect or history of the return from Babylon. Say what you will about the highly poetical form into which the Prophet has undoubtedly thrown his fervid thought, still there is the thought beneath the form which clothes it. If it would be a degrading mistake to resolve this passage into a mere description of some vast engineering operations; if valleys were not literally to be filled up, and mountains were not literally to be levelled, something, at any rate, was to take place in the moral, social, or political world which should correspond to this vigorous imagery. And that something was to interest, not merely the Jewish race and their heathen neighbours, but the whole human family: "All flesh shall see it together." It is clear that the particular, local, temporal deliverance melts before the eye of the Prophet— as, gazing on it, he describes it—into a deliverance, general and world-wide in its significance, extending in its effects far beyond the limits of time. The Deliverance of deliverances is before him. He sees the great escape from bondage, of which all earlier efforts at freedom were but shadows; he sees it afar off, the pathway of mankind across the desert of time from the city of chains and sorrow, whereof Babylon was the earthly type, to the city of freedom and glory imaged in Jerusalem. And thus it is that the Evangelists so unhesitatingly apply the passage to St. John the Baptist. St. John was, as we Christians know, the immediate forerunner of the Deliverer of humanity; St. John, as a hermit of the desert and preacher of repentance, supplied, by his life, the connecting link between the literal and spiritual senses of the prophecy;

St. John, gathered up in himself, embodied and represented the ages of prediction and expectation; he was the mind of the Old Testament in a concrete form, laying down its office and proclaiming its work of preparation finished, when the Reality Which it foreshadowed had come.

Now although, as we were reminded by our Bishop on Ash-Wednesday, it is a fatal error to speak as if the providences and the Being of God were a mere reflection of the wants and thoughts of man; although Redemption is an objective fact, the primary motive of which we may reverently but surely say was the setting forth before the moral universe the glory of the divine Redeemer; yet still it is true that the Only-begotten Son of God, "for us men and for our salvation, came down from heaven." It was not that He modified His original plan by adapting His Incarnation to the necessities of a fallen race. These necessities were foreseen; they entered into, they determined the form of His advent, which thus combined our dearest interests with His highest honour. He came indeed that, even by His deepest humiliations, He might set forth God's attributes of righteousness and love. But He came also at the voice and pleading of our deep necessity; He came to die for all, because, as His Apostle says, all were dead; He came for His own glory indeed, but also because if He had not come, we must have perished irretrievably.

Accordingly, the preparation for His advent was rather of a character required by our need than essential to His glory or to His personal triumph. It has indeed been said by a great military leader of modern days that the first condition of success in a campaign is the possession of accurate information as to the strength and movements of the enemy. Certainly, the Captain of our salvation was already furnished with all necessary information; He had measured from the depths of His eternity the foe whom He would conquer, and the shame and penalty to which He would submit. But, if man is to share in His Victory, man must be prepared for His advent, man must be educated for the blessing in store for him. Unless man is to be redeemed as he was created, without any consent or co-operation of his will; unless he is to be saved as if, instead of being a moral agent, he were a tree or a stone, man must enter in some measure into the designs of his Benefactor; the way of the Lord must be prepared, the highway of our God must be laid down in the desert of man's moral and intellectual wanderings.

I. It is plain, my Brethren, that our subject is too wide to admit of any but a very partial treatment. Let us then observe that the most necessary element of this preparation for the Victor was to convince man that he needed redemption by a heavenly friend and conqueror. We know that in this country no political measure that really touches the interests of the people can receive the sanction and the force of law, unless the people themselves are convinced that the evils which the measure purposes to remedy are substantial and not fancy evils. No legislative genius on the part of the minister can dispense with this condition of success. If the country is not convinced that the measure is necessary, the minister must take measures that will produce this conviction. He must hold meetings; he must make speeches; he must write dissertations; he must deal in dry statistical demonstrations and in vehemently passionate appeals; he must set in motion all the complicated machinery of political agitation and enterprise which may be at his disposal. Supposing him to be himself satisfied of the necessity of the measure in contemplation, this is nothing more than his duty to his country: he would fail of that duty if he could neglect to diffuse, according to the best of his power, that amount of political information which is necessary to his success.

You will not understand me to be saying that here we have a strict and absolute analogy to the sacred matter immediately before us; because it is plain that the correspondence fails in a most vital particular. We all know that the enactment of a new law in a free country is, in reality, the act not of the legislature but of the people: the legislature is only the instrument of the popular will. But the Redemption of the world is in no wise the work of redeemed man: Christ is the One Redeemer in Whose redemptive triumph man could have no part save that of accepting and sharing its blessings. Yet this deliberate acceptance of Christ's Redemption by man is of vital necessity to man; man is not saved against or without his will to be saved; and it is therefore of the last importance that he should understand his need of the salvation, which he must desire and accept.

Now what was the evil which Christ was to conquer, in man and for man? It was sin. Sin is the one real evil. It is certainly worse than pain; since pain may become a good. It is certainly worse than death; since death is only the effect of sin and may be the gate of freedom. It is worse even than the devil; since it makes the devil to be what he is. The devil would be powerless, and death would have no sting, and pain would be unknown, if it were not for sin. But sin is not a thing always palpable to and recognised by the sinner. It is like the peculiar atmosphere in which we pass the great part of our lives here in Oxford. Looking down upon our homes from the top of Shotover, we see the thick damp fog burying this city and valley beneath a shroud of unwholesome vapour; but here in the streets of Oxford we scarcely observe it hanging in the sunlight, except when it becomes excessive in the depth of winter. Sin is just such a mist as this: it is a fog, a blight, impalpable yet real, about us, around us, within us. It bathes our moral life on this side and that, and withal it blinds us to the fact of its existence. If man would take a true measure of sin, he must be lifted out of it; he must ascend to some moral eminence whence its real character will be made plain to him, and where he may form strong resolutions to close with any offer of deliverance and escape from its importunity and thraldom.

Now such an eminence was supplied in early days by the gift of a moral law; and, first of all, let us, like the Apostle, in some passages of his Epistle to the Romans, use that word in its large inclusive sense, for any form of moral truth presented to the soul of man. Of all moral law God is the Author. And moral law was the chosen messenger whom He sent before the face of His blessed Son, to reveal man to himself, and to produce in man a conviction of the need of a Redemption. Of this gift of law there are plainly very various measures. To the heathen He gave the natural law, the law of conscience, the perception that there exists a real distinction between right and wrong, often going hand in hand with grave mistakes as to what was right and what was wrong. And yet still in a true sense, the Gentiles, although not having the Jewish law, "were a law unto themselves, which shew the work of the law written in their hearts, their conscience also bearing witness, and their thoughts the meanwhile accusing or else excusing one another[a]." To the Jews God gave the gift of law in a form far higher and brighter. The Decalogue was, the Bible says, "written by the finger of God on two tables of stone." It came not from within the consciousness of Moses, it was presented to him from without; although Moses at once recognised, he could not but recognise, its truth. It came from God, as an external, independent revelation; it did not gradually arise in one or in many minds by any process of gentle, imperceptible growth; Scripture represents it as having been flashed forth from heaven, suddenly, visibly, amid the rocks of Sinai. No law which God had placed in the conscience of any heathen people could compare with the revelation received by Moses; it shed an illumination upon human life, it held up a standard of human action, it implied an idea of the awful sanctity of its Author, with which nothing in heathendom was correspondent.

Undoubtedly, my brethren, the primary purpose of law is, that it should furnish a literal rule of conduct, or, in other words, that it should be obeyed. But if law is not obeyed, it may yet have a use which no wise man will underrate. It may lift up the voice of a perpetual protest against the society which falls short of its requirements, or which violates it, or which is in a fair way to forget it. In this case, instead of being a standard which creates a sense of satisfaction, by being fulfilled, it becomes an ideal, which stands in humbling, because reproachful, contrast to the dull, sluggish life which is so far below it, or which outrages its behests. Now this, according to St. Paul, was a main function of moral law, both Jewish and

[a] Rom. ii. 14, 15.

Gentile, before the coming of Jesus Christ. Even among the heathen, the natural law, which came from the light of conscience, prescribed a standard, which utterly condemned the actual life of the heathen. St. Paul enumerates a long catalogue of sins which the Pagan philosophers knew to be evils, no less certainly than did the Apostle of Christ, but which the Pagans nevertheless continued to practise on an organized system, and in a very business-like way[b]. And although the Jews "made their boast in the law," that is to say, were not merely thankful for possessing so full a revelation of God's will, but compared themselves, self-complacently, with other peoples to whom that revelation had not been made, still, the question was, did they obey it? "Thou that preachest a man should not steal, dost thou steal? Thou that sayest a man should not commit adultery, dost thou commit adultery? Thou that abhorrest idols, dost thou commit sacrilege? Thou that makest thy boast of the law, through breaking the law dishonourest thou God[c]?" To this question one answer only was possible: the Jew 'rested' in a law which he did not obey. The revealed Law was his; it was his, not to bless but to condemn him; it was his to convince him that if he had a brighter light to guide him than the Gentile, he also incurred a proportionably deeper guilt by neglecting it. Thus both Jew and Gentile were concluded to be under sin; and in different degrees, it was true that by the law came the knowledge, the blessed salutary knowledge, of such sin[d]. More than this, the presence of the law irritated the activities of that hidden mischief which it revealed. "I had not known sin," says St. Paul, speaking in the name of human nature, "but by the law: for I had not known

[b] Rom. i. 24—32. [c] Ibid. ii. 21—23. [d] Ibid. iii. 20.

lust unless the law had said, 'Thou shalt not covet.' But sin, taking occasion by the commandment, wrought in me all manner of concupiscence. For without the law sin was dead. For I was alive without the law once; but when the commandment came sin revived, and I died. And the commandment which was ordained to life, I found to be unto death[e]." We are not to suppose that the moral law was really creative of evil which did not exist before: since the law comes from a Holy God, and is itself "holy, and just, and good." But although the law did not add to the stock of existing evil, it drew the unsuspected latent sin of man forth into the daylight; it irritated into intense vigour the principle of opposition which, even when dormant, is ever so strong in sinful human nature, and which shews itself, under the irritation, in its true light as sin. The law was like those remedies in medicine which rid us of a disease by bringing it to the surface, or, as we say, by precipitating it; it forced man to see what he really is, and to forget what he had fancied himself to be. " By the law is the knowledge of sin."

This was the function of the law of nature in the Gentile world, and of the law of Sinai, in a much higher degree, in the Jewish world. It was like a light shining in a dark cavern, and the forms of sin around were lighted up by it with a lurid glare, which only did them justice. The graceful wickedness of heathendom, the profound hypocrisies of the Jew, when confronted with this heavenly light, fell into their place. The law tore off the mask; it penetrated beneath the skin; it pierced even to the dividing asunder of soul and spirit, and of the joints and marrow. It ranged the great palpable sins of the Jew and of the Pagan in their due order of ma-

[e] Rom. vii. 7—10.

lignity: but it did more than this, it put sin before man in a light which made its burden, as we say in the Communion Service, altogether intolerable.

For what is moral law, viewed in its essence? It is the proper Nature of God, the perfect Moral Being, unfolded in language. This language shews the bearing of God's Nature upon the life of man. The moral law is not an arbitrary code which God might have made otherwise, or might have left unmade altogether. God, being such as He is, could not have made the law otherwise. For God, I repeat, is the Moral Being: He is Love, He is Truth, He is Justice, He is Sanctity. He cannot legislate in contradiction to His nature: He cannot but express His nature in His legislation. If He had been a mere all-comprehending Intelligence, a mere all-producing, all-controlling Force, He might have ordered what He has proscribed, and have forbidden what He has commanded. As it is, God's freedom is bounded on this side of His action. God might have made a natural universe very different from that which we behold: the heavenly bodies, this earth and its tenants, the rocks, the plants, the animals around us are what they are only because He freely willed them to be so. He was under no kind of constraint when He gifted you and me with reason, and denied reason to the quadrupeds and the birds: He might have reversed the order of His gifts; He might have withheld them. But having surrounded Himself with creatures capable of moral action, He could not devise a law which should deny the truth of His own necessary Nature; He could not but legislate as He has. Moral truth, like truths of pure mathematics, is co-eternal with God: it must always have been true that "truth is a virtue," as it must always have been true that "things which are equal to the same are equal to one another." And if moral or mathematical truth is thus co-eternal with God, it cannot be something independent of God, a second, self-existing truth alongside of, and external to, the one original self-existing Being; it must have been, it must be, an integral part of God; a law or element of the Divine Nature. And therefore God could never have said, "Thou mayest bear false witness against thy neighbour; thou mayest commit adultery; thou mayest steal; dishonour thy father and thy mother," any more than He could have said, "Thou mayest have other gods but Me." Given a created moral agent like man, and God cannot but bid man obey the rays of moral truth which stream from His own uncreated Essence. Such rays are the law of an undivided love and homage towards Himself in all its bearings of reverence and worship, the law of honour due to parental authority, the law of reverence for the sanctity of life, the law of responsibility in the transmission of the deposit of life, the law of truth applied to property, and to language, and to the hidden desires of the heart. God would not be God if He could have reversed these commands; the Decalogue is God's nature veiled beneath the language, and adapted to the facts of the life of man. And therefore a violation of the moral law is not the setting aside of a capricious order; it is the violation of a law which streams forth necessarily from God's holy Nature, being such as It is; it is a resistance to, a negation of, God's Nature; it is, without any exaggeration, an act or state of will which, if produced indefinitely, would annihilate God.

This may enable us to enter into the meaning of the two words for sin which, both in the Hebrew and the Greek languages, most perfectly unveil its fundamental character. These words call it 'a missing the aim or mark,' i.e. the mark or aim of the life of man. My brethren, what is that aim? In other words, why were we sent into this world at all? Now, if we sincerely believe in a Creator to whom we owe simply and altogether the gift of existence, must not each one of us answer the question as follows? 'I was sent into the world to conform my will to the Will, that is, to the holy Nature of my Maker, so far as I know it. I was not sent here to please myself, but to please the Being Who gave me life. Had I been the unaccountable product of some stray chance, the upshot of some unintelligent force which in its capricious fertility happened to throw off into existence such a singular and complex result as are my body and my soul, although wholly without the consciousness and purpose of doing so, then I might have concluded that I owed nothing to any being but myself, and I might have lived selfishly to enjoy only the fleeting existence which belongs to me. As it is, I believe in a God Who has created and Who owns me: and being thus created and owned by God, being His creature and His property, it is my business, my first and truest business, to live for Him, to bring my will into harmony with His. I am unlike the lower creatures around me, unlike the beasts and the plants, unlike the forces of nature, the heavenly bodies, the sun and the stars, in that they must of necessity obey Him. But that I might obey Him freely He has enabled and bidden me to love Him. To make room for love there must needs be liberty. The earth incessantly revolves around the sun, but the earth does not love the sun. Why? because liberty is of the essence of love. The earth cannot deviate from her orbit. That I might render to my God the free service of love, He has given me the power of refusing obedience. It is my duty, then, and my happiness to obey a law which is not any arbitrary product of His will, but which results from the essential truth of His nature. Each deed, each word, each thought which embodies such refusal misses the end for which I exist; it is that unutterable and radical misfortune which I recognise as sin.'

Such is the language of a soul which believes in God, and is withal illuminated by moral law. In this high atmosphere of truth the glosses by which sin's true nature is too often disguised slough off and fall away. The soul is in the wilderness listening to the voice which is preparing the way of the Lord before her. In such bracing solitude, face to face with truth, men do not conceive of sin as of a mere external fact, or series of facts, of such and such quantity and bulk, which can be witnessed by the human eye, or felt or measured: sin is seen to be more than this, namely, a posture or warp of the will. In the presence of divine law men do not imagine that sin is limited to violations of human law: since human law does not always enact what is absolute right; and it never pretends to enact all that is right, or to prescribe all that is wrong. Human law rarely enacts more than is necessary for the well-being of society, it does not attempt to legislate for the wellbeing of individual men. A false and misleading standard in the things of the soul is human law; it is one thing to keep out of the police-court, it is another to be at peace with God. Taught by the law of God, men do not substitute for the stern, unyielding rule of right and wrong, the plastic, varying, untrustworthy standards of 'good taste' and 'bad taste.' No doubt virtue is always really in good taste, and vice is always in the worst taste possible: but this judgment is formed according to an absolute standard of taste which identifies it with moral truth, and not according to that relative and local standard which is 'good taste,' perhaps, with you and me at this hour, and may be 'bad taste' with our successors twenty or thirty years hence. As a matter of fact, stern virtue is often voted by 'good taste' to be awkward and graceless, while there are forms of polished ungodliness which 'good taste' welcomes or at least condones. When men understand that the law of God, in its essence, is the Nature of God, they do not think lightly of sin: they do not think of an act of sin as of an act which has no consequences; they do not think of it as of a scar that heals in a few days, or as of a force which spends itself, or as of a colour which fades. They see that wilful sin necessarily empties the soul of God, and leaves it as the bed of the ocean might be without the waters which can fill it. They see that sin introduces a state which does not terminate until it be reversed by an act as definite as the act which introduced it. They see that sin, as being the moral negation of God, is not a fancy of the human mind, but a real fact in the universe, and that to have sinned wilfully is, until a man repents, to be in a state of spiritual death.

Such was the discovery of his moral state to man effected by the presence of moral law. But the moral law did more even than this. It shewed man that there was an original warp and deficiency in his nature which made sin welcome, and conformity to moral truth difficult to him. My brethren, we here touch upon a truth of revelation which is especially repugnant to some forms of modern thought, and which at first sight may appear to be in conflict with our notions of natural justice. "It is hard," say you, "that I should inherit a sinful nature because my ancestor sinned some six thousand years ago. I will not believe the dogma which tells me this." Very well, you reject the dogma: you make up your mind that you are born holy. But now that you have parted with revelation, hear what nature tells you. You had, we will say, an intemperate great-grandfather, and he has transmitted to you an enfeebled constitution. You are scrofulous, or you are consumptive, or you have a heart-disease, or you are rheumatic: and this comes to you with the blood you inherit. You may say that your body ought to have been created like your soul, by a separate act of the Creator, which might have detached you from this entail of misery and pain. Still, my brethren, you cannot seriously revise the creation: and it is not common sense to resist unalterable facts. Here revelation is perfectly at one with nature. Physical evil is transmitted from sire to son; and a like transmission of forfeiture of moral good is equally certain. It is plain that God deals with us men, partly as individuals, but partly also as one great family, I had almost said as one vast organism, with laws, wants, privileges, of its own. Certainly the sin which Adam transmitted was not anything positive, such as a poison, or bad blood. When Adam sinned, he forfeited that original righteousness, that robe of grace and beauty with which his Creator's mercy had endowed him in Paradise, and he simply could not bequeath what he himself had lost. But as the gift of righteousness which he had forfeited left his natural passions in rebellion, and his faculties dislocated and deranged, so he passed on to his children a nature thus enfeebled and disordered, and open to the solicitations of evil, and disinclined for goodness. It was in mercy, not in judgment, that he was still permitted to transmit the gift of natural life. God would not deny to millions the gift of life because the sin of an ancestor brought with it an inheritance of weakness and of shame.

From the first God gave a promise of coming salvation. But still man felt his weakness, he felt his inherited degradation, the ruins of his earlier greatness survived in his intellect and in his heart to tell the tale; and when the moral law cast its clear, bright light upon his conscience, a David exclaimed not merely, " I acknowledge my own fault, and my sin is ever before me," but also, "Behold I was shapen in wickedness, and in sin hath my mother conceived me."

Thus it was that among the most gifted race of the ancient world there was observable in poetry and generally in art a vein of deep melancholy, which faintly confessed inward misery, and yearnings for a blessing which had once been promised. Nature herself was in sympathy with man; death was an inexplicable mystery in the world of the All-merciful; the whole creation groaned and travailed in pain together[f]. The great mystery of pain, which is not solved in our chemical laboratories and museums, hung heavily on the thought of the ancient world. Paganism, too, had its sense of violated right, and its wild attempts at expiatory sacrifice; and, under a higher sanction, the courts of the tabernacle and of the temple reeked with the blood of victims, ever reminding the people of the covenant that they bore an accumulating load of sin of which they could not discharge themselves. Prophets reiterated, expanded, enforced the teaching of the lawgiver; they gave it sharpness of point and particularity of application, thus stimulating into keener consciousness the national and individual sense of sin. Psalmists poured forth strains of penitence which pierce the souls of all who have felt the presence of moral evil within them, even in Christendom, revealing as they do, the

[f] Rom. viii. 22.

majesty and the searching convicting power of the divine law. This was its function: "By the law is the knowledge of sin." But it discovered what it could not relieve, it quickened anxieties which it could not allay, it generated hopes and yearnings which it could not satisfy. It taught men that there is a divine life, but it did not give them strength to lead it; it furnished mankind with an ideal, but it left the ideal high out of human reach. In the presence of law man knew what he ought to be; he knew that he was not what he ought to be; he yearned for a pardon which should free him from guilt, and for a strength which should lead him heavenward. The law, said St. Paul, is like a Greek slave who leads his master's children down to the school of the teacher who will instruct them, but the slave has done his work when he has left them at the door. The law is a schoolmaster to bring us unto Christ.

II. Therefore the discovery of man's deep need was accompanied by another discovery, the revelation of a Deliverance. The hopes of man are as ancient as his despondency. At the gates of Eden was given the promise that the seed of the woman should bruise the serpent's head. We interpret that promise, and rightly enough, in the light of its fulfilment. But when it was given it might have seemed vague, and capable of many interpretations; nothing was certain from it except that man's deliverance would in some way be wrought out through humanity itself. Around this promise all the faith and hope of the earliest ages gathered, and from this point prophecy gradually narrows and becomes definite as it proceeds to unfold its true interpretation, until at length, when Isaiah and Zechariah had spoken, the whole life and sufferings of Jesus Christ had been written by anticipation. To Noah it was revealed that the promise would be realized among the posterity of Shem; it was then still further narrowed to the descendants of Abraham. Here we encounter the selection of a peculiar people, who were to be privileged, not for their own sakes, but for that of the human race at large: "In thee shall all nations of the earth be blessed." When Jacob foretells the coming Shiloh, it appears plainly that the deliverance is to spring from a single tribe, nay more, from a single person. When Balaam speaks of the star of Jacob and of the sceptre rising out of Israel, we see that the Object of his vision will have the glory and power of a monarch. Moses himself predicts a Prophet to Whom Israel will hearken; a coming Teacher, not an order of teachers, Who will reveal the mind of God with a truth and fulness unknown before. But it is in the age of David that these scattered rays of hope are brought into a focus. There we meet first of all with the limitation of the promise to David's family; next, with the sacred name Messiah, so pregnant with meaning and with hope; thirdly, with the guarantee of an endless kingdom, such as no merely human descendant of David could have been supposed to inherit. In these prophecies the hopes of the world are sometimes commingled with the more immediate hopes of Israel; a human king is in the foreground of the prediction, and yet the prediction contains much which would be applicable to no earthly monarch. Here we encounter the two aspects of the life of Messiah,— His life of humiliation and suffering, and His life of exaltation and glory. Each of these is described with great particularity. One psalm is a picture of Christ triumphing over the rebellious heathen, another of His victory over death, another of His sufferings upon the cross eventuating in the conversion of the world, another of His mediatorial reign of glory. The Davidical outline, if it can with justice be called an outline, is filled up by the later prophets. Isaiah describes Messiah's supernatural birth, the features of His ministerial action, the long line of titles, divine and human, which reveal His Natures and His office, the details of His humiliation and sufferings. Daniel determines the exact period of His coming, and the character of His kingdom; Zechariah anticipates even minute incidents of the history of the Passion; Malachi closes the Jewish canon with a prediction of His forerunner.

In so vast a field we must limit ourselves, and I would press upon your attention this one observation as being in harmony with the present course of sermons, and as being altogether borne out by the facts of the prophetical literature :—the coming Christ of prophecy is always a conqueror. So patent, indeed, is this note of victory in the prophetic utterances respecting Him, that the Jews materialized it in accordance with their political hopes, and expected a military leader who would defeat the armies and rival the empire of Rome. The Jews were fatally wrong in this perversion of the promises which they had inherited; their eyes were blinded by their political passions, and accordingly they missed the true Deliverer when He came. But they were right in laying emphasis on the victoriousness of the Messiah, though His victory was not to be won by material force. In prophecy Christ is pre-eminently the victor; He conquers ignorance as a teacher, or He conquers sin as an example, or as a victim; He conquers moral rebellion from a heavenly throne; He conquers death in the chambers of the dead. It is sin, sin in itself, sin in its consequences, over which He triumphs; the iniquity of us all is laid upon Him, yet " He shall see His seed and prolong His days." He is not more victorious in the prophecy of Daniel, when He is brought to the Ancient of Days and there is given to Him a throne and dominion, and a kingdom, than He is in the twenty-second Psalm or in the fifty-third chapter of Isaiah, when He sees of the travail of His soul and is satisfied, and when all the kingdoms of the nations, converted by His self-sacrificing love, worship the true God. Prophecy, in short, is one long hymn in His honour, and it salutes Him across the abyss of intervening centuries as the Hope of humanity advancing to achieve its freedom. "Thou art fairer than the children of men; full of grace are Thy lips, because God hath blessed Thee for ever. Gird Thee with Thy sword upon Thy thigh, O Thou most mighty, according to Thy worship and renown. Good luck have Thou with Thine honour. Ride on, because of the word of truth, of meekness, and righteousness; and Thy right hand shall teach Thee terrible things[k]."

Brethren, have we,—have you and I—any true part, at this moment, in that victory of the Conqueror, which the moral law led man to yearn for, and which is the theme of prophecy? Surely here is a question for Lent. Lent should be to us something more than a name in the Calendar. Lent is no mere fancy-observance of serious and old-fashioned Churchmen, who live by their Prayer-book; no mere relic of the thought and feeling of a bygone age. It is rooted in the moral needs of human nature; it speaks to every thinking man; it recalls us to the consideration of undying truths. It speaks of truths which, certainly, we never should forget, but of which it is well that we should be periodically and solemnly reminded. "Strip

[k] Ps. xlv. 3—5.

off," it says to each of us, "the disguise which hides thee from thy real self; and dare to look thy God in the face. One day thou wilt die; thou wilt pass into another world alone. Art thou now what thou wouldest be then? Dismiss fancy-standards of goodness, and look higher and deeper for the measure of thy life. Cease to move in a vicious circle of morals, even as thou wouldest not knowingly reason in a vicious circle of argument. Cease to judge thyself by a self-made measure: cease to legislate when thou shouldest be standing at the bar of judgment. Dare to meet the law of moral truth. Thou art not a Pagan, that thou shouldest be judged by the twilight of thy natural conscience: thou art not a Jew, that thou shouldest read thy acquittal or thy condemnation in the two tables of stone. Thou art a Christian: Christ's Cross was traced once upon thy forehead: Christ's Creed and Law have sounded in thine ears, and been confessed by thy lips: nay, Christ's Nature has been given thee, whether thou retainest, or hast lost, that gift of gifts. Thou art a Christian: and as a Christian thou must be judged, thou must judge thyself, by a standard which Pagan and Jew knew not. The Sermon on the Mount, the law of love and of sacrifice—this, this only, is thy positive standard. Thou art not by rights a slave, grudgingly yielding the stinted meed of service which just escapes punishment: thou art by inheritance a son, upon whom a generous Spirit of freedom has descended, that thou mayest obey the law, not of bondage but of liberty. The fruits of that Spirit are love, joy, peace, long-suffering, gentleness, goodness, faith, meekness, temperance: against such there is no law of reproach and condemnation. Before thou canst bear these fruits, thy lower nature must be trodden down and killed. They that are Christ's have crucified the flesh with the affections and lusts. This is the standard of the conqueror of sin: is it thine?"

Is it so, my brother, that thou hidest thy face, and wouldest fain sink to the very dust for fear and shame? Is it so, that not in the New Testament merely, but in the Decalogue, not in the Decalogue alone, but in the light of thy natural conscience, thou tracest the sin of Judah written with a "pen of iron and with the point of a diamond?" Dost thou hear the sentence which Eternal Justice must needs utter against thyself? Canst thou only tremblingly murmur: "The enemy hath persecuted my soul, he hath smitten my life down to the ground; he hath laid me in the darkness, as the men that have been long dead. Therefore is my spirit vexed within me, and my heart within me is desolate." "Out of the deep have I called unto Thee, O Lord: Lord, hear my voice." Then take heart, for it is well with thee: thou, too, art ready for the Advent, or rather for the return of thy Lord as conqueror of thy spiritual enemies. There would be but little hope for thee, if thou wert still dreaming of thy personal excellence: as it is, thou knowest that thou art "miserable, and poor, and blind, and lame." Cease, then, from thy despondency: He, thy Redeemer, calleth thee. If thou wilt, He is ready not merely to forgive the guilty past, but to bid thee rise with Him to newness of life. Ask, and it shall be given thee: seek, and thou shalt find. His Cross and Wounds, His words of pardon, His robe of righteousness, His sacraments of grace and power are within thy grasp. He hath not given thee over unto death; thou shalt not die but live, and declare the works of thy conquering Lord.

SERMON III.

The Victor, manifest in the Flesh.

ROMANS viii. 2.

"For the law of the Spirit of life in Christ Jesus hath made me free from the law of sin and death."

THERE is a remarkable likeness in these words of St. Paul, to those with which St. John concludes the preface to his gospel. When the Evangelist has told us of the Word becoming flesh and dwelling amongst men, he goes on to tell us how the fulness of that incarnate life passed, "grace for grace," into the life of men. And he contrasts this "grace and truth," which came by Jesus Christ, with the law which came by Moses, and which, though itself a divine gift, brought no such gift of life as that which God has bestowed upon us in His only-begotten Son.

This idea of a life which saves us, thus contrasted with the idea of a law which has no power to save, is evidently the same with that which St. Paul sets forth in our text, and which appears so frequently in all his writings.

The "fulness" which St. John declares that he received from the Incarnate Word, is the same with that "spirit of life in Christ Jesus" which St. Paul declares has made him "free from the law of sin and death." The "law" which St. John contrasts with "grace and truth," is that same law which St. Paul pronounces too "weak through the flesh" to effect his deliverance. Those whom St. Paul describes as walking "not after the flesh, but after the spirit," are those same "sons of God" whom St. John describes as "born not of flesh, nor of blood, nor of the will of man, but of God."

One and the same idea, taught them by one and the same revealing Spirit, is evidently present to the mind of each Apostle. It is the new idea of the deliverance of humanity, by the transforming power of a life, which Christianity has added to the older one of deliverance by the efficacy of an atoning death.

But though they teach thus the same truth, and almost in the same words, they have arrived at it by very different ways.

St. John begins with the contemplation of the Divine nature which was made flesh. He tells us of "the Word which was in the beginning with God, and was God;" how "by Him were all things made," and how in Him was that life which is the only light of men; and so he comes down to the idea of that Word becoming flesh and dwelling amongst men, and of their receiving from Him grace and truth. St. Paul, on the other hand, begins by contemplating that human nature which the Word came to redeem. He studies it in its infirmities, its sins, its struggles, its aspirations, and from these he rises to the conception of that new life which it is to gain from the Incarnate Word.

St. John defines for us our Saviour; St. Paul describes the salvation that we need. St. John, as it were, ascends to heaven to bring Christ down to us; but St. Paul descends first into the very innermost parts of his own being, and learns what manner of a Saviour he must be, who is to deliver him from the evil that he finds there. The one, with his calm, deep, solemn words, so full of mystery, and yet so full of love, seems like some angel messenger just lighted upon earth, strong and beautiful, the track of his path through the heavens still bright with the light from the throne of God. But the other, with his words of passionate agony, his all but despairing cry for a deliverer, seems rather like some traveller through a dark, trackless forest, earth-stained, toil-worn, wounded by each entangling thicket through which he fights his way; but fighting it still resolutely, desperately, through every difficulty, on to the light and freedom that in his darkest hour he still believes he yet shall reach!

And we, brethren, who stand beneath the Cross where these two ways meet—we who hear the divine harmony that these two widely-differing tones make as they blend in their utterance of the Church's hymn to Christ as God—we feel how ill we could afford the loss of either. We feel how inestimably precious to the Church is this twofold aspect of this great central truth of all her faith and all her life.

In the great theological definitions of St. John, we possess a fixed standard of dogmatic truth, by which we may test and correct our erroneous and imperfect conceptions of it. We see how the Spirit of God has lifted up in these for all time a sculptured likeness of our Lord, that stands clearly and sharply defined, high above the distorting mists and fogs of error and ignorance and doubt, that are ever rising in the lower region of our fleshly nature. On the other hand, in this close, searching analysis of that very nature by St. Paul, in the clear light that he has thrown upon its essential elements, in the profound perceptions he gives us of its needs and desires, we have another safeguard against false and imperfect views of the Incarnation. For in thus deepening our idea of the deliverance that we need, he prepares us for deeper views of the deliverer who is to accomplish it. As we think of the one, so we may be sure will we always think of the other. We cannot have shallow views of our own nature, and deep and true views of the person and work of Christ. All creeds and dogmas notwithstanding, each one of us sees just that Christ, and no other, whom he believes himself to need.

He who believes that humanity requires or can receive no higher powers than its own, will see in Christ no more than a man like himself. He who believes that all it requires is knowledge of virtue, will see in Christ a great moral Teacher and no more. He who believes we need only a revelation of certain doctrines necessary to salvation, will see in Christ an inspired Prophet and no more. He who believes that we need a great example, will see in Christ no more than an ideally perfect Man. But he who feels that the deliverance he needs is something far deeper than any one of these, or all of them together; he, at least, is so far prepared to accept the idea of an incarnate Saviour, that he can see that all those other Saviours men picture to themselves are no Saviours for him. Those reeds shaken with the wind; those prophets merely; nay, even those more than prophets, which they are ever going out into the wilderness of barren speculation to see, have no attraction for him; they fail, one and all, to satisfy the need of his soul.

And on the other hand, he who does rightly believe the Incarnation of Christ, may gain fresh reasons for his faith as he sees how the deepest parts of his nature answer to this deepest mystery of his creed; as he sees how the Incarnation which he believes can alone supply that salvation which he needs.

It is this aspect of the subject I ask you to consider to-night. I ask you to approach it—not as St. John does, by the way of revealed dogma—but as St. Paul did, by the way of human experience. Let us forget for a moment, as we are so often exhorted to do, the definitions and dogmas of our religious books, and question only the soul within us, which we are told we theologians will not listen to, but which, if we would only suffer it to speak, would give us a religion deeper and truer than any of our creeds.

We take, then, this Word to-night, not as a revelation of dogma, but as, what all admit it to be, a revelation, the deepest and truest we possess, of human nature. We turn to those who in this book have revealed for us the needs, the sorrows, the struggles, the aspirations of their souls. And of these we will question those and those only who have not yet learned our dogma of the Incarnation, those who, believing only in God the Father, have not yet learned to believe in Jesus Christ His only Son our Lord.

The Bible reveals for us the experience of three men, who, above all others, seem to have been tried with the question, of the deliverance of humanity from evil. The first of these is Job. In him we see humanity contending with evil in its simplest and least terrible form, in that of outward circumstance only. The troubles of Job come to him altogether from without. They fall on him as so many blows dealt him by another's hand; he has not caused them, he can neither resist nor escape from them. They sweep over him, wave after wave, and he drinks their salt bitterness, and dreads the death they threaten; but he has no more to do with their coming or their going than the drowning man has with the rise or the fall of the tide. Like that other sufferer from a God's displeasure, who embodies for us the highest conception that uninspired man ever formed of this conflict of humanity with evil, conscious of his utter helplessness, conscious too of his integrity, he lies the victim of omnipotence, chained down to suffer all that resistless power can will to inflict.

But for the Hebrew Prometheus there is both an agony and a hope unknown to the Greek. Job cannot, like the sufferer in the Grecian drama, take refuge from his torment in defiance of his tormentor. He cannot conquer his conqueror by the calm, resolute power of the indomitable will that, mastering agony by endurance, lifts the righteous suffering man above the unrighteous cruel God. On the contrary, the very sharpest pang in all Job's trial, is the temptation to think and feel thus towards his God. For the God of Job is a good God, is the Father of his spirit, whom he has loved and served all his life, and he trembles at the thought that his sorrows and his sufferings should cause him to lose his faith in this God. At the thought of this a chasm seems to open beneath his feet, an abyss of evil into whose dark depths if he should once sink, he feels he is lost for ever. For then the evil that before was all external to him, would have become a part of him; his very inmost self would have become enmity against God. Then would he have "cursed God and died" —died the eternal death of a spirit, that, separated from the true centre of its life and light, wanders hopelessly away into the blackness of darkness and despair for ever! Well might Job tremble and shudder as he saw this form of evil approaching him. It was the very shadow of his tempter!

But as this temptation comes from without, deliverance from it would seem to come most naturally and easily by a change in those outward circumstances that cause it. Let God only "take away His rod from him;" let Him "cease to terrify him;" let him be no longer driven to and fro by the blast of His displeasure, like "a dried leaf driven by the wind," and all will be well. This phantom of atheism that vexed and terrified his soul, had its home in that dark dungeon of outward circumstance in which he lay; it will vanish in the broad free light of open day. Give him back his old prosperity, his honoured, useful, happy life; make him the man he was in times past, when the eye that saw him blessed him, and the ear that heard him witnessed to him, and the old peace of his spirit will come back again; the world would be no longer in alliance with his flesh to assault and hurt his soul.

The deliverance, then, that Job desires is a deliverance from the evil that is in the world,—a victory *for* him, *for* his flesh, over the world. His Redeemer would be a restorer, a healer of outward nature, one who would stand for him and with him on this earth, and enable him "*in his flesh* to see God," and to see Him as his Father. This salvation from outward evil is that which humanity, in the lower stages of spiritual development, alone can conceive of. This is the salvation of the heathen,—whose saviours were always heroes or gods who did heroic deeds, slaying the monsters that assailed men, destroying, that is, some one of the outward ills that flesh is heir to. And this is the salvation of too many Christians, whose only idea of a Saviour is of one who has saved them from some penalty attached to sin, and who will some day make a great change for the better in their outward condition, by translating them to heaven.

And now we turn to question one who had in large measure that very deliverance from evil that Job desired. Wise, learned, rich, powerful, he tells us that he applied all the treasures of his wisdom, and power, and wealth, to fashioning for himself a paradise on earth. No foreign war or domestic revolt broke the peaceful prosperity, or dimmed the glory of his reign. He tells us too what came of it all,—"vanity and vexation of spirit." He tells us how he "hated all his labour," how he hated his very life. Yes! Solomon in his glory was ready, as Job was in his misery, to curse the day that he was born! And with better cause. The evil which Solomon endured was worse far than that which afflicted Job. The torture of satiety, the loathing of all things that comes on him who has enjoyed all and wearied of all, is more intolerable far than that which the sharpest pain or sorrow brings, for it is hopeless. For the sufferer from this form of evil, no change of circumstance can bring relief, there is for him no good, and he is, therefore, in terrible danger of believing that there is no God. The atheism of pleasure is far darker, far deadlier, than that of pain.

Solomon's experience, then, of evil is more profound than that of Job. He sees what Job did not see, that this evil is not in the world, not in circumstances, but in himself. It is because he has not "kept from all his eyes desired," because he "has not restrained his heart" from all the joys it cared for, because he gave himself too greedily to the enjoyment of the "good that

God had given him under the sun," that he is thus weary and jaded and wretched. If he had enjoyed only in moderation, if he had observed the time and the mean that God had appointed for all things, he would have been happy. And accordingly, "the conclusion of the whole matter," the remedy for all the evil he has known, is self-restraint, obedience to those laws and ordinances of God which condition our enjoyment of this world. "Fear God, and keep His commandments, so shalt thou come forth from them all!"

Solomon's idea of deliverance from evil is Law—a system of checks and restraints upon the appetites and passions of man, sanctioned indeed by the highest motives, by those of religion. His ideal deliverer would be a lawgiver, a prophet who should reveal to men new precepts, and enforce them with powerful sanctions. His heaven would be a paradise, but one in which flaming swords turning every way should keep men from all forbidden fruit. This is victory, not *for* the flesh but *over* the flesh. This is the salvation of the heathen moralist and the philosopher; it is the self-conquest they are always speaking of, the conquest of the lower part of our nature by its higher and better part, the triumph of the man over the beast in us. This is the salvation of the ascetic, whether heathen or Christian ; the man who—believing that the seat of all evil lies in the material part of his nature, the flesh in its lowest and most literal sense—seeks his deliverance from it in the mortification, the torture, the very death of that rebellious flesh that opposes itself to his higher will. This is the salvation, too, of a far lower school, that coldly moral school of Christian teachers, who think of Christ as the Son of God come down from heaven chiefly to give us an "authoritative sanction" for natural religion, to prove

His mission by miracles, and to reveal to us new motives why we should restrain from evil, new reasons, in His clearer revelation about heaven and hell, why we should fear God and keep His commandments.

And now we pass to another; to one who has tried this remedy of Solomon's; one who did indeed fear God with all the reverence of a devout soul, and keep all His commandments, as he believed, with all the strictness of a resolute, self-denying will; one who was "as touching the law blameless." And what is his experience as to the deliverance that law, even divine law, can effect from evil? He tells us how utterly it failed to deliver him; how it became to him rather the deadliest and most terrible of evils; how when it "came" to him, when he really came to understand what law was, the sin he once thought dead in him revived in the presence of this restraining law, and "slew him," so that the commandment ordained to life he found to be unto death.

For this law, this external restraint, with all its awful power, wakes in him another and a mightier law,—"a law in his members," a law of lawlessness, an intolerance of all restraint, a force of resistance that no mechanical power of repression can restrain. And this lawlessness, this impossibility of subjection to law, is the very bent of his nature. It is his very self, and yet it is not himself. There is in him another and a better self that delights in law, longs to obey it, and yet cannot enable him, the whole man, to obey it. And so he finds within him a terrible strife, a conflict between good and evil, light and darkness, law and lawlessness, conscience and will, that rends him in twain, and forces from him, in the misery that it wakes in every fibre of his moral being, the exceeding great and bitter cry—"Oh! wretched man that I am, who will deliver me!"

And yet this is not all; within this deep there is a deeper still. The fear of Job falls on the soul of Paul with tenfold dread. He sees that this evil bent of his nature, this lawless impatience of all law, is really "enmity against God" who is the Author of law; is the expression, therefore, not only of the lawlessness but the godlessness of human nature; is in its essence atheism, the refusal of the created will to own the will of the Creator; the miserable desire to be its own god and its own law. True, he has not consciously yielded himself to this godlessness of his nature. True, St. Paul in his inner man still contends against this law in his members. But what if it should prevail at last? What if this carnal enmity rise up higher and still higher from his lower nature and invade, first his mind, then his conscience and his soul? What if the last utter victory of flesh over spirit change this miserable dualism in him into a yet more miserable unity, a unity of evil? What if the spirit within him, yielding itself to this double assault of passion and of understanding should consciously, wilfully, deliberately, rebel against the God whose existence it can never cease to be conscious of? What if the "enmity," that in the lower nature shews itself only in the preference of the creature to the Creator, should in the higher nature develope itself into its completed and perfect form, the burning hatred of spirit against spirit—the fiend's choice—Evil, be thou my good! This were death, the worst of deaths, a life in death, a hideous consciousness of the dissolution that comes after death, the wild anarchy of all the elements of our nature when the life that held them all in check is gone! This was the death that Job saw afar off; but which Paul saw already begun within him, and that seeing he shuddered, and groaned, and cried out for a deliverer, a Saviour.

To such a cry what answer shall we make? Shall we tell this troubled soul that "humanity will be saved from evil when it once understands the great laws of its own being, and of nature?" or shall we tell him that there appeared in the world "a great Prophet who revealed a sublime system of Ethics," and enforced it by new and awful sanctions? or that this Prophet was "a sublime soul,—an ideal man,—a glorious example of what humanity may attain to?" Nay, shall we even tell him that this man's death procured forgiveness of his sins, and admission to heaven after death?

With what a sad, bitter smile, would this sufferer listen to such miserable comforters. You talk to me of law, he would say, of understanding, obeying law. I understand what law is far too well already. Law is my curse, my misery; it is law that is driving me to despair and to madness. I need no miracles to convince me of the authority of law, no prophet to tell me to fear God and keep His commands. I do fear Him, and I cannot keep His commandments, and my dread is, lest I cease to fear Him, lest the law within me drive me to outrage and defy Him. What is it to me that your perfect Man has realized the idea of humanity, unless He can make me to do so too? What is that pure, noble, perfect life to me, but an object of hopeless envy? And even your sacrifice for sin, your forgiveness for the past, it is much, very much; but it is not all. It is forgiveness, but it is not deliverance. It may save me from the hell hereafter, but I need salvation from the hell in me now. I need deliverance from myself, from that human nature in which I feel my misery lies. Not law, but the righteousness of the law; not restraint, but a nature that shall need no restraint; not a healing of this or that evil symptom in this or that part of my nature, but a cleansing of my whole nature from that original taint of lawlessness in its life-blood that fills its very veins with poison; not a victory *over* the flesh, but a victory *in* the flesh; a new law of life that shall free me from the law of sin and death; a new principle of unity in my nature by which, instead of the spirit growing carnal, the flesh shall grow spiritual; this, and this alone, can save me.

And now that we have learned, from these cries of the human soul in its conflict with evil, what is that deliverance that alone can satisfy its needs; let us turn to those despised dogmas, those abstract theological definitions which we are told have no relation to our real life, and see what they have to tell us. Let us hear again the answer of St. John to the question of St. Paul! "The Word was made flesh, and dwelt among us," "full of grace and truth." "And of His fulness have we all received, and grace for grace." What is it that these words tell us, as we read them in the light of that human experience we have been studying? They tell us of "flesh," of a human nature, really, truly human, dwelling amongst men, subject to all the conditions of their human life, bone of their bone, flesh of their flesh, but filled with "grace and truth." A humanity in which there was no untruth, none therefore of that unhappy falseness to its own ideal, that taint of evil ever making it untrue, which we feel in our nature, and yet which we feel is no part of our nature, is unnatural, is fatal to it. They tell us that in this sinless flesh we see, not a perfect Man merely, isolated from all other men by His very perfection, but human nature, the manhood taken into God, and becoming, by its union with the eternal all-creating all-sustaining Word, a new source of life for all men, capable of imparting itself to all, so that of its fulness all men may receive, and "grace for grace." They tell us how this nature may become our nature, making us perfect with its perfection, true with its truth.

Is not this the deliverance and the Deliverer that we need? Not a Prophet merely, not an example merely, not an ideally perfect man; but a new humanity, a new life for men. Yes, the dry creed, the abstract dogma comes down, like Him whom it defines, and dwells amongst men, and we see that it too is full of grace and truth, as it reveals to us the glory of the salvation and the Saviour, that alone can satisfy the soul of man!

But is this idea of a triumphant humanity really fulfilled in the life of Christ? Was His life really so true, so perfectly sinless as we say? The sinlessness of Christ cannot be fully treated of in one, or in many sermons; I can but suggest one line of proof, and yet one which seems to me very weighty. I ask, in the first place, what was the aim and desire of the whole life of Christ? It was undoubtedly righteousness,—perfect, unswerving obedience to the will of His heavenly Father. From the first word of His, that declared that He "must be about His Father's business," to the last word, that proclaims His Father's work is finished, one thought, and one only, seems to be the ruling passion of His life—"to fulfil all righteousness." Those even who will not admit that He succeeded in this, must admit that He ever aimed at this.

That law of righteousness, then, which St. Paul recognised as the ideal of His being, was never absent from the mind of Christ. How comes it, then, that in all His life, there never once appears the slightest trace of St. Paul's consciousness of failure to realize that ideal? In no one of all His utterances concerning Himself, in none of the records of His temptations, His trials, His fears, His hopes, His most secret and inmost thoughts and prayers to God, do we ever find so much as a hint of His own imperfection. Never once do we hear from Him a prayer for forgiveness, a cry for deliverance from sin. How is this? Surely it is he who has the highest ideal, who is ever most distressed at His own failure to realize it. Surely we might have expected that the soul, which in all human history has the highest and loftiest ideal of holiness, will feel most keenly its own failure to be holy. How is it, then, that we find in Him only the most calm, serene, unbroken, self-approval? How is it that the spiritual perceptions of Jesus seem at once so much higher, and yet so much lower than those of all other men? How can He be at once so far beyond St. Paul in His ideal of perfection, so far below Job in the consciousness of His own imperfection? Is His love for holiness an hypocrisy, or His belief in His own holiness a miserable delusion? Is this life of Christ, that for eighteen centuries has drawn to it the admiring gaze of friends and foes, nothing after all but the strangest and saddest of all moral monstrosities, the most inconceivable mystery of united contradictions? And if it be not this, what else can it be, but just the realization of that very ideal of humanity, the fulfilment of that dream of righteousness that has haunted every righteous soul that ever sighed, and sighed in vain, after perfection—a human nature freed from all taint of evil, all flaw of imperfection—a victory and a victor manifest in the flesh?

But if this human nature of Christ were truly sinless, was it exposed to trials such as ours? Did this sinless humanity really triumph over all those forms of evil to which we are exposed? Let us see. The temptations for our human nature from without, infinitely varied as they are in outward circumstances, are all of two kinds,—the temptation of Job, and the temptation of Solomon. The trial from want, or from enjoyment,—the creature desired, or the creature possessed,—are the two forms under one or other of which man is ever tempted to prefer it to the Creator.

Turn now to the life of Christ, and we shall see Him, in the first place, through the whole of it exposed to the temptation from the possession of the creature. The whole world of nature was His absolutely. All outward circumstances would change at His bidding. It needed but a word from Him to form round Him and His a charmed circle, within which, want and pain and sorrow should be unknown. He, "the preacher," might indeed have been "King in Jerusalem"—king of an earthly paradise, of which Solomon in all his glory never dreamed. And yet He never would do this. Never once in all His life does He use His miraculous power to save or serve Himself; never for any other purpose than the working out of His Father's will and His own mission. His was a life-long self-denial; a life-long restraint upon desires of the flesh, in themselves pure and noble. Here is that submission to law, that reverence for divine command, that subjection even of the sinless will of the creature to the higher will of the Creator, that breathes itself in His last prayer, and brings Him forth from His last trial, but of which His whole life was but one long expression: "Father, not My will, but Thine be done." *This is victory over the flesh.*

But on the other hand, the temptation of Job was His likewise. The world was potentially His;—actually, He had not where to lay His head. The King and Lord of nature walked this world of His, a weak, weary, troubled man, in perils oft, in sorrow always; for the sorrows of all others were His own, by that intensity of sympathy which made Him truly one with us. Bowed ever with the burden of others' woes, the horror of others' sins; weeping with those that wept, burning with those that were offended, righteously indignant with all wrong, tenderly sympathizing with all who suffered, and yet isolated, too, like Job, by the intensity of His suffering, from those who, even though they loved Him, could not understand Him; He "the perfect and the upright man," whom Job alike in his righteousness and his sufferings foreshadowed, He appears the true type of Humanity, tried by suffering, and conquering by endurance. For it is by endurance that He does conquer. He does not escape from suffering, He submits to it, and in submitting triumphs. His is the mastery, the only true mastery over outward circumstances; that which comes not from the power to change, nor even merely to endure, but from the power to subdue; the power to make that which is outwardly unfavourable minister to the inner life. He conquers want by wanting, weariness by wearying, pain by suffering, grief by grieving, death by dying. All these outward ills are His ministering servants; out of all these His life gathers its growth, its perfection. They minister the elements of His glory, as the earth, and the sun, and sky, bring forth the glory of the perfect flower from the life of the seed submitted to their influences. This is the victory *for the flesh*, the only victory that really overcomes the world. This is the victory that comes from that faith which places man above and beyond the world, which makes humanity the lord of nature and time and change and chance, because it makes all these subservient to that life, which has its source not in the creature, but in the Creator, not in the world, but in God!

Compared with this one great life-long victory for humanity, this conquest over all outward circumstances, those other occasional miraculous conquests of His,— those victories, not of endurance, but of change of circumstance, that strike us so much at first—seem infinitely smaller conquests. We might conceive of our being able to work all these works, and greater than these, and yet gaining no real victory. What would it avail us, though we could turn stones into bread, and water into wine, if our gluttony and intemperance made us slaves to the food and the wine we had miraculously produced? What would it avail us, if we could heal diseases with a touch, and recall the dead with a word, if the health we regained, or the loved we called back, were to us more than God, were sources to us not of life, but of death?

Is not this the mistake, the sad mistake, man is ever making, when he imagines that his discoveries of the powers of nature are giving him power over nature. The truth is, that they are all of them giving nature increased power over him. These new forces in nature which man discovers, as we apply them to the uses of human life, What do they do for us? They quicken the pace at which we must all live. We must live now faster, harder far than our fathers did. Steam and electricity are our masters, not we theirs. We are like hands in some great factory,—the faster the wheels revolve, the faster, the more unremitting is our work to keep up with them. Do the wires of our telegraphs flash happier tidings than we used to gain by slower conveyance? Do the swift trains on our railways bear happier, nobler, truer men, than those we look on with such pity for their want of our knowledge of the resources of science? If not, circumstance is our master, and conditions our life as much as theirs. Which do you think is most truly lord and master of outward nature, he who could by one wonder-working word bind the old world and the new with such a link as binds them now, or he who could hear with patient trusting heart, with calm unshaken faith, the message those wires might send him, that all he loved, and all he possessed in life were gone? The world might be the master of the one; the other would be the master of the world!

It is this mastery that our Lord has won for us; the complete triumph of humanity over circumstance, by its complete emancipation from the power of the creature. It is the reversal, point for point, of the victory won through the creature by the enemy of man over humanity. That was the subjugation of man to the dominion of the creature, which tempting him through the flesh, overthrew the lawful rule and supremacy of the spirit. This is the subjugation of the creature to the dominion of man, by the restoration of the lawful supremacy of the spirit over the flesh. That was the victory of the world, through the flesh, over the spirit. This is the victory of the spirit, through the flesh, over the world!

And it is this double victory of spirit over flesh, and of spirit and flesh over the world, that constitutes the claim, and proves the right, of His victorious humanity, to that universal kingdom that He won by it. He who would be king must first be priest. The consecration of self-sacrifice must precede the consecration to rule and dominion. The humanity that is to rule all things must first prove itself incapable of being ruled by any. It is because He did so, because in Him humanity has shewn itself proof against its twofold trial from the creature,—the trial of want and of possession, freedom and enjoyment—because He the Second Adam has passed victoriously through both the trials of the first,—the trial of the garden and of the wilderness—the world under the curse, that brings forth still the thorns of care and sorrow, and that other world too, that might at His bidding have brought forth for Him nothing but delight,—for this it is that God has highly exalted Him, has given Him His Name above every name, has given Him the sceptre that He has proved may safely be intrusted to His hand, has raised Him to that throne which even He could not ascend, unless He first descended to its lowest steps on earth, and step by step, from suffering to suffering, from victory to victory rose to its seat in heaven, to dwell there far above principalities and powers and dominions, crowned, because victorious, Man!

And these victories are all to be ours as well as His. That nature in which He has conquered, that flesh which has thus in Him won its twofold triumph, He has told us, He has come to give to us. Given for us first as our atoning Sacrifice, but given to us then as our sustaining life, this is that bread of life that came down from heaven, which he who eats of shall live by for ever!

He tells us how that flesh, that human nature shall dwell in us, victorious in the law of the spirit of its life over that law of our fallen flesh that lusteth still against the spirit. He tells us how, by the power of that life, because He lives, we shall live also, victorious *over* our flesh, victorious over its lawlessness, crucifying it, mortifying its deeds, bringing its high thoughts into captivity, and learning still obedience by the things that thus we suffer, growing still in our inner, our new nature, more and more like to Him, as that holy thing born in us of the will of God, and of the power of the Holy Ghost, grows to the fulness of the stature of the man Christ Jesus, until at last we too become victorious *in* the flesh, until His last victory won for the flesh is accomplished in us. This new humanity of ours, proved like His in its double trial with the creature, conquering, unlike Him, with many and many a sad defeat intermingled with its victories, but conquering still by enduring to the end, shall win of His infinite mercy the crown He won of right, the crown of life, perfect and eternal; shall pass with Him through its last struggle, know its last pain, sigh its last sigh, win its last victory by suffering, and then freed for ever from its burden of the sin that He condemned, in the likeness of sinful flesh, changed to the likeness of His glorious body, by the working of that power wherewith He subdues all things to Himself, shall reign with Him for ever!

Yes, victory in the flesh, victory over the flesh, victory for the flesh,—we need all three,—we need to see all three united in one and the same Saviour. There are times when our thoughts rise not beyond a victory for the flesh. Times when in the sharpness of some sore trial, in the weary heart-sickness of some life-long sorrow, we only desire to flee away and be at rest; we see through our blinding tears but the far-off gleam of the walls of the golden city, and think how blessed to be within their safe defence, where pain nor grief can ever come! And, again, there are times when, with all our treasures round us, in the full enjoyment of all that this life can give, we feel that this is not enough, that there is a higher, truer life than this, and that if we cannot attain to it, we have lived and loved in vain, and that without this, the joys of heaven itself would pall upon us at the last, and we should loathe the monotony of its rest, and the eternal quiet of its peace. Then we rejoice to think of that other, that higher victory won for us, the victory for the spirit over the flesh, the victory by which the soul of man can rise from the enjoyment and love of the creature, to the enjoyment and the love of God, and finds its true life in Him. And yet, again—when we have won this victory, when in the might of this love we have accomplished some act of self-sacrifice for Him we love; when the spirit of the crucified one has triumphed over the flesh, has mortified, has crucified it even—we feel by the pain of crucifixion that this victory is won only by a strife and an effort so exhausting, that heaven itself were dearly purchased, if it were to be held by such incessant warfare as this; we feel that its crowns of glory were but a mockery, if those who wore them still bent beneath the cross. Then we rejoice to see that other victory won, the victory not only over the flesh, but in the flesh. The victory not of the Cross and Passion, but of the Resurrection and Ascension. The victory, final and complete, of the law of life in Christ Jesus, that even now as it works within us gives us the seal of our inheritance of the saints in light, but which then, fulfilling itself at last in all our nature—body, soul, and spirit—shall give us all the fulness of the gift of God, eternal life in His eternal love!

"Thanks be to God who giveth us *this* victory," through our Lord Jesus Christ!

SERMON IV.

The Victor, exalted to His Throne.

DANIEL vii. 13.

"I saw in the night visions, and, behold, one like the Son of Man came with the clouds of heaven, and came to the Ancient of Days, and they brought him near before Him."

THIS is one of those passages which has been made a ground of objection to the authenticity of the book of Daniel, on account of the clearness with which it seems to enunciate a great Gospel verity, and so to anticipate the ideas and belief of a later period. It occurs at the conclusion of the vision in which, under the similitude of the four beasts, was represented to the prophet the successive rise of four great monarchies. The immediate object of the whole revelation was probably to encourage the Israelites in their captivity, and, at the same time, to prevent them in their impatience from expecting a speedy coming of the kingdom of the Messiah; monarchy after monarchy would arise, throne after throne would cast its shadow over the nations. The lion, and the leopard, and the bear, and the beast—diverse from and stronger than the rest, Chaldæan, Persian, Greek, Roman, must each run their course, bringing apparently no nearer the hope of Israel; but ("though it tarry wait for it, because it will surely come, it will not tarry always"), suddenly a change passes over the prophetic ecstacy. The field of vision is no longer this earth. From the weary spectacle of human power rising but to fall, gathering its strength only to be broken, Daniel is transported to the sight of a sublimer sovereignty: "I beheld till the thrones were cast down and the Ancient of Days did sit; whose garment was white as snow, and the hair of His head like the pure wool; His throne was as the fiery flame, thousand thousands ministered unto Him, and ten thousand times ten thousand stood before Him. I saw in the night visions, and, behold, one like the Son of Man came with the clouds of heaven, and came to the Ancient of Days, and they brought him near unto Him." The passage was uniformly interpreted by the Jewish doctors of the person and kingdom of Christ. And the language is too plain to be otherwise expounded, hence the attempt to get rid of its testimony as a great Messianic prophecy by bringing forward the authorship of the chapter to a later date. But, indeed, clearly and magnificently as these verses speak of Christ upon His throne, they do not stand alone in the Old Testament. This prophecy of Daniel is by no means an isolated one. Blot it out of the Sacred Volume, and the great truth of Christ's exaltation to the right hand of power would still remain written down unmistakeably in the prophetic Scriptures. For example the 110th Psalm is no less distinct: "The Lord said unto my Lord, Sit Thou on My right hand until I make Thine enemies Thy footstool." Our blessed Saviour has Himself applied these words to His own person and kingdom; and it is obvious, if interpreted of Him, that they point to the same event as those of Daniel,—the bringing near of the glorified humanity of the Redeemer into the presence of the Father, the seating it upon the throne of heaven thence to exercise a special dominion, until all things shall be subdued under His feet.

Now it is this crowning and enthroning at the right hand of the Father, of the Man Christ Jesus, which is the subject proposed for our thoughts to-night. It is told us historically in the words of St. Mark: "So, then, after the Lord had spoken unto them, He was received up into heaven, and sat on the right hand of God." It is predicted, not in one but in many passages of the Old Testament; not exclusively, although with a wonderful sublimity, in that which we have read to you for the text: "I saw in the night visions, and, behold, one like the Son of Man came with the clouds of heaven, and came to the Ancient of Days, and they brought him near before Him."

Upon this exaltation of Christ we now go on to speak.

I. And first as to the truth itself.

Now the peculiarity of both the prophecies alluded to, that of the text and that in Psalm cx., consists in this, that they represent the act of exaltation, as seen within the veil. We are all familiar with this act, so far as it was beheld from the earth: "He led them out as far as to Bethany, and lifted up His hands and blessed them. And it came to pass while He blessed them, He was parted from them, and a cloud received Him out of their sight." The natural eye could see no more of that great enthroning of humanity. The steadfast upward gaze could not penetrate the veil between the two worlds. It is just here that the prophetic Scriptures supply what is wanting; that which the natural eye could not see, the inner consciousness of the old prophets in ecstacy had been privileged to behold.

Daniel had gazed upon the scene within the everlasting doors, to which all that passed upon the Mount of Ascension was the introduction, the in-coming into heaven of the Son of Man. David, in the spirit, had caught the mystic words, the high welcome of the eternal Father: "Sit Thou on My right hand."

Now when we turn to the doctrine involved in these passages, we are at once brought across that which has in all ages formed the great trial of men's faith, "the twofold nature of Christ." It has not passed away, that old probation of the Church. In early ages, when the remembrance of Christ Jesus upon the earth was comparatively fresh, when His gracious accents still lingered as it were upon the air, the temptation was, in the vivid perception of His perfect Manhood, to drop or hold loosely the truth of His eternal Godhead. Hence the multifarious heresies which vexed the primitive Church, agreeing mostly in the attempt to find, as it were, some place for the Redeemer which should satisfy in a measure the great things spoken of Him and yet make Him less than God. Resisted by Athanasius, condemned by the Council of Nicæa, that old Arian heresy has never wholly died out, although it may have changed its form. And one of the evils which it has produced has been this, that in their very zeal to maintain the proper Godhead of their Lord, true and devout souls have sometimes lost sight comparatively of the equally great truth, "that He is perfect man." This second error finds place chiefly in regard to our blessed Lord's present life in heaven. Let us examine it for a few minutes to-night.

The grand question between the Church and the world, philosophy and faith, is this—"What is Christ now?" To the world He is a great Benefactor of the past, a mighty Teacher who fulfilled His mission and departed, leaving His mark (by the wisdom of His precepts and the purity of His example) upon all future times. To the Church He is a living agent still, not by the influence of what He was, but by the force of what He is. But now let us advance a step farther. Amongst those who have a full belief in the present life and action of Christ, there is often, nevertheless, a singular vagueness of idea as to the nature of Him who sitteth upon the throne. The tendency is the opposite of that which sapped the faith of the early Church, for it is to lose sight of the perfect Manhood of Christ Jesus in His session at the right hand of the Father, in the adoration of Him as one with the Father in majesty and glory. As of old they were slow to recognise God upon earth in the form of a servant; so now are believing minds dull in appreciating the reality of "man in heaven" amidst the ineffable glories of Almightiness. The majesty of His estate has, to them, extinguished the verity of His human nature[a]. Probe such men closely, and you will find that whilst they repeat day by day the sentence, "He ascended into heaven," they do not give its full force to the truth that He who ascended was Very Man, the same in form and substance as He had been upon the earth, that the Incarnation was not for a few years but for evermore; so that what is seen now in the depths of the light inaccessible, as the object of adoration to angels and archangels, is the body of man. Probe, I say, the popular belief closely, and it will be found that when people think of Christ as He is now, they think of Him as possessing a sort of compound nature, in which the power of God and the

[a] Hooker, bk. v. 55.

tenderness of man are commingled, not as preserving still (in heaven as on earth) our human nature in all its integrity.

Now it is observable how very careful Holy Scripture has been to impress upon us this truth of the enthroning of Christ's Manhood at the right hand of the Father. How careful and minute, in this respect, is the narrative of the Ascension. The walk to Bethany, the lifting up of the hands, bring before us emphatically, at the last moment before its withdrawal, the reality of Christ's human body. Again, the words of the angels: "This same Jesus, who is taken from you into heaven, shall so come in like manner as ye have seen Him go into heaven." We seem to have here an accumulation of words to emphasize the great verity of the preservation of the Lord's human body, age after age, within the unseen world to which He has gone, until the time comes when in it unaltered He shall stand again upon the earth. Accordingly, the vision of St. Stephen revealed Him within the innermost glory in human form. In the midst of the light which blinded him for awhile, and which is no doubt rightly interpreted as being the flashing out of the Shekinah of the Divine presence, St. Paul is thrice distinctly said to have seen Jesus. So with regard to that title in the text, "the Son of Man;" our Lord Himself, adopting it, perhaps, from this very passage of Daniel, uses it no less than fifty-five times, and always in reference to two opposite subjects—either His extreme humiliation, or His coming upon the cloud; as though to unite together in thought the depth and the height, the manhood and the glory. It does not follow from all this that the human body of our Blessed Lord has undergone no change. We are told of a wondrous transformation to pass upon our own bodies at the general resurrection. And so the record of our Lord's sojourn upon earth during the great forty days, gives intimations of His resurrection body being endowed with powers which it had not before. And it may be that in many ways beyond the reach of our capacity, hath that body been further glorified, since the heavens received it. Still the truth remains as St. Augustine stated it—"Make thou no doubt but that the man Christ Jesus is now in that very place from whence He shall come in the same form and substance of flesh which He carried thither,—and it behoveth us to take great heed lest while we go about to maintain His glorious Deity, we leave Him not the true bodily substance of a man [b]."

But this is not all. The perfection of Christ's Humanity implies that He had a human soul as well as a human body; and so you find in the history of His human life two distinct series of sensations attributed to Him, those which belonged to the body—hunger, thirst, weariness; and those appertaining to the human soul—wonder, sorrow, friendship, fear. It is not, as again an ancient heresy suggested, that the Divinity possessed and animated, instead of a soul, the sacred Body of Christ. His manhood was complete, consisting both of human flesh and human soul.

And yet more,—even as the spear and the nails left their impress upon His sacred form, so that after the resurrection their marks were visible to St. Thomas; so did the trials and temptations of life exercise their own proper influence on His soul, shaping it to sympathy, and giving to it a distinct individuality. There is a sense in which our Blessed Lord is Man, the representative of the entire race,

[b] Quoted by Hooker, Eccles. Pol. v. 55.

belonging to no age or country, but equally akin to all; there is another sense in which He is to be regarded as a Man, in soul and body as created, and as acted upon by the circumstances of life, possessing a perfect individuality.

And thus we may approximate to the great truth before us. The Victor on His throne!—He who in His human nature was tempted, but in vain; who knew alike bodily anguish and travail of soul, has transferred Himself with that body and soul to the highest heaven. The Ascension was no laying aside of His human nature, like a garment whose use was over, but the exaltation of that nature above the angels. Hence the meaning of those passages which speak of His having, for the joy which was set before Him, endured the Cross. To His human soul, the crowning and enthroning of His human nature was a real support and encouragement, when the waterfloods closed over Him. Hence, too, the fulness of the assertion, that God hath made us sit together in heavenly places in Christ Jesus, because our nature in its perfectness is already there in Him. Hence the literal fulfilment of all those prophecies of the perpetuity of the throne of David, because He who rules now, and will rule to the end the Israel of God, is as truly the offspring of David as He is the Son of God. Hence in heaven, not on earth, is the full mystery of the Incarnation revealed. That God should dwell below in the form of a servant for three and thirty years, baffles our minds; that He should reign for ever in heaven above, as in the earth beneath, Perfect Man, is a more astounding mystery still. Yet is this the doctrine of Christ's exaltation. Within the innermost tabernacle of Deity, upon the sublimest height of God's holy hill, amidst the unknown shapes and dazzling ministries of the everlasting, Scripture bids us recognise the form of a Son of Man brought near to the Ancient of Days.

II. And now pass on to some of the results of this doctrine.

(1.) Upon it, we may at once say, depends the true conception of the dispensation under which we live. The language of Scripture speaks almost invariably of the Church, as the Church of Christ, the kingdom not of the Father, but of the Son. Now the importance of this distinction grows out of the truth that Christ upon His throne is still Man. If that Manhood which He assumed when conceived by the Holy Ghost of the Virgin Mary, and in which whilst upon earth He baffled all the assaults of the great enemy was laid aside at the Ascension, or in any degree absorbed and lost in His Divinity, then would it be a distinction of small moment, to speak of the Church as His Church, rather than the Church of the Father. It is the continuance of His proper humanity, now that He is on His throne, which gives the importance to the distinction. Because He is Man still, therefore in no figure of speech, but in a literal sense, may we speak of Him as watching with peculiar care as our Elder Brother over the destinies of the Church, overruling, guiding its conflicts, sympathizing with its saints, the same in His relationships to them and to us, as to the Apostles of old, when visibly going in and out among them. He, which without our nature could not on earth suffer for the sins of the world, doth now also by means of that nature exercise dominion with a true, a natural, and a sensible touch of mercy. And hence we may see the true character of the book of the Acts. Its position in the sacred volume is a peculiar one. Midway it stands between the Gospels and Epistles, apparently belonging to neither. What is its voice to the Universal Church? Why this; to set forth the continued life and action of the Man Christ Jesus now that He is withdrawn from sight; to stamp upon all time this truth, that the dispensation of the Gospel since the Ascension is under the rule of the self-same Being who first preached it. St. Luke regarded the Acts only as the second chapter of His Lord's life. So in the outset he speaks of his former treatise as being a narrative of what Jesus began to do and teach, that action and teaching being still carried on, as he designs next to shew, from within the veil. Accordingly, the choice of Matthias to fill the vacant Apostleship is represented as referred to Christ; the outpouring of the Holy Ghost as His gift. He appears to Stephen in his agony. He stands by St. Paul at every great crisis of his career, pointing the way in which he should go. Under all the outward instrumentality of apostolic zeal, missionary journeys, councils of elders, we are made to see clear and distinct the Lord Jesus, the same in form and character as we beheld Him in the Gospel narratives, Himself essentially unchanged by the change from earth to heaven, from humiliation to glory.

(2.) The enthroning of our Blessed Lord as Perfect Man, exactly meets the necessities of our own nature. That which constituted the great fascination of idolatry was that it offered to the worshipper, as an object of worship, something which his mind might in a measure grasp. The demand of the Israelites, " Make us gods to go before us," was the cry of man yet in the infancy of his moral training, unable to lift up his heart to God as a Spirit. And their whole after tendency to idol worship sprang out of the same craving for something which they could more perfectly realize in the object of their worship. Similarly, it has been observed, that the practice of invoking the Blessed Virgin and the saints began to acquire strength just at the period when controversies as to our Lord's Divinity died out. The triumphant vindication of His proper Godhead, led by a natural re-action to comparative forgetfulness of His perpetual Manhood; and as the mind accustomed itself to contemplate Him only in the Majesty of the Godhead, it began to crave for intermediate intercessors whom it could realize more perfectly. The error in either case arose out of the same instinctive yearning of men's souls for something akin to humanity in the Being to whom recourse was to be had for sympathy and aid. Now it is just this desire of the soul which is met and satisfied by the Catholic doctrine of the session of the Man Christ Jesus upon the right hand of the Father. Assure me that He is there whom Thomas felt and handled, in all the integrity of Manhood, in the Body which was pierced, with the Soul that knew fear and sorrow, and you give me something upon which my mind can repose when lifting itself up feebly and wearily to the eternal world; "Touching the Almighty we cannot find Him out," but in becoming incarnate, and that for ever, He has Himself scattered the cloud that is around Him, and drawn near to the creature whom He desires to draw upward to Himself.

(3.) We may observe how the whole sacramental system of the Catholic Church harmonizes with this same doctrine of Christ's continued Manhood in heaven. What a double character runs through the dispensation under which we live! As in the two great Sacraments, so in minor ordinances, spiritual agency is veiled ever under outward forms. In prayer, in preaching, in the Bible itself, it is the same. Something outward and visible, something human and tangible is the veil of a power operating beneath, which is more than human. In scarcely any religious act are we left to purely spiritual operations. Fanaticism revolts against this order. Intellectualism derides it. But is there not a wonderful harmony between these laws of the kingdom and the nature of the King! We are, so Scripture tells us, within the mediatorial empire of the God-Man. He who is the Head of the Church is not divine only, but human likewise. The visibility of the kingdom is but a projection upon this nether world of the visibility of the King above. The whole system of ordinances, uniting so incomprehensibly the earthly and the heavenly elements, independent, yet inseparable, does it not find its proper crown and consummation in that mystery of mysteries, the second Person in the Trinity incarnate upon His throne.

Here then are some of the results of the exaltation of our human nature to the right hand of power. Other and profounder consequences there may be which we cannot fathom. How far the whole course of this world is modified, the trials of each individual soul affected by the truth that the Head over all things is Perfect Man as well as God, we shall probably never know until that mysterious moment when the mediatorial kingdom shall be resigned. But inasmuch as all these things are not theological fictions, but realities; a reality, the bringing near of a Son of Man to the Ancient of Days, and His receiving the dominion; a reality, the delivering up of that dominion to the Father when the end shall come, therefore must we believe that our whole existence, even although we know not how, is coloured by the fact that we are under the sceptre of One who is Flesh of our flesh. So, from generation to generation, the majestic session is prolonged. Age after age casting up its own forms of evil, and He, the Victor on His throne, gathering out of each His own triumphs, working through each the counsels of His will, in His twofold nature laying His hand at once upon the infinite and finite, meeting the upward yearnings of His people, giving its own special character to their warfare and their worship, and so preparing them, by an intermediate discipline, for that life where no longer through a Mediator, but face to face, they shall see God, and know as they are known.

Finally, let us from this whole subject gather fuller, deeper convictions of the solemn character of our own earthly lives. Doubtless there are difficulties in apprehending this prolonging of the great mystery of the Incarnation;—but this difficulty is only one instance among many of the tendency to banish the supernatural to the realms of the past or the future. Past and future, it has been said, are great words, and the changes which they necessarily involve are so strange and eventful, that it seems not inconceivable that the work of redemption should have been wrought in the one, and that the hour of judgment should await us in the other. The marvels of the manger bed are softened down in the dim distance, and the terrors of the great white throne are swathed in the thick folds of ages not yet unrolled. But the doctrine on which we have spoken knits up our modern lives, even as the lives of the Apostles were knit up of old with the supreme miracle of all, making the Incarnation itself a contemporaneous fact. It may be a teaching hard to receive. Yet herein lies our strength against temptation, our incentive to high purposes and holy living. The more we realize the truth of our own lives being interwoven even now with the sublimest mysteries of God, a portion already of the invisible and the eternal, the more mean in our eyes will become the pleasures of sin, the more determined and the more hopeful our resistance to the evil which compasses us around.

SERMON V.

The Victor, on His Throne, the Object of Divine Worship.

—•—

REVELATIONS v. 11—13.

"And I beheld, and I heard the voice of many angels round about the throne and the beasts and the elders: and the number of them was ten thousand times ten thousand, and thousands of thousands; saying with a loud voice, Worthy is the Lamb that was slain to receive power, and riches, and wisdom, and strength, and honour, and glory, and blessing. And every creature which is in heaven, and on the earth, and under the earth, and such as are in the sea, and all that are in them, heard I saying, Blessing, and honour, and glory, and power, be unto Him that sitteth upon the throne, and unto the Lamb for ever and ever."

ONE is the Church of the redeemed; one is their God, their Lord, their Head; one Spirit knits the whole in one, pervading all, filling each separate member according to the capacity of each to receive Him; endowing each with his own special gifts, and in all diffusing the love, the wisdom, the holiness, the righteousness of God. One they are, because He who pervades all the whole mystical body of Christ—militant, expectant, triumphant,—is one and indivisible.

And as they themselves are one through the in-oneing Spirit, so the Object of their being, their bliss, is one; only, that while our praises, and thanksgivings, and intercession ascend together to the eternal throne, those above, being already perfected, need no prayer for graces for themselves. No *Miserere* can mingle with their unceasing, endless Halleluias, save for us in our pilgrimage, whom they long to be brought safe through, to swell the sweet concord of redeemed praise.

One, also, is the object of their worship; one only object can there be of divine worship, Almighty God. This was the fundamental central doctrine of the old law: "The Lord our God is one Lord[a];" "And thou shalt love the Lord thy God with all thine heart, and with all thy soul, and with all thy might. Thou shalt fear the Lord thy God: Him shalt thou serve, and to Him thou shalt cleave, and swear by His name[b]." This doctrine our blessed Lord emphasised at the threshhold of the Gospel, when He rebuked His bad rebellious spirit and dismissed him from His sacred presence with the words, "Get thee behind Me, Satan. For it is written, Thou shalt worship the Lord thy God only, and Him only shalt thou serve[c]." "Since then," says St. Augustine[d], "we serve both the Father and the Son and the Holy Spirit with that servitude which is called *latreia*, and we hear the law of God enjoining that we should shew this to no other but the Lord our God only; doubtless our one and only God is the Trinity Itself, to which, one and alone, we, by right of piety, owe such a servitude." Hence it was rightly objected to the Arians that, owning (as they did, and as Socinus did in later times) that our Lord was an object of divine worship, and yet holding God the Son to be a creature, they were, in fact, idolaters. It would have been but the revival of the old Polytheism within Christianity.

[a] Deut. vi. 4, 5. [b] Ibid. x. 20. [c] St. Matt. iv. 10.
[d] c. Serm. Arian, c. 29, Opp. viii. 643.

"Who told them," says St. Athanasius[e], "'Abandon the worship of the creation, and then draw near and worship a creature and a work?'" "They," said another[f] as to the heathen, "whereas they ought to have worshipped the true God, offered the divine honour to the creation. To this censure are they too liable who call the Only-begotten Son of God a creature, and yet worship Him as God. For it were due, either if they call Him God, not to rank Him with the creation, but with God who begat Him; or if they call Him a creature, not to offer Him divine honour."

Nor, plainly, does the humility of the Incarnation make any difference herein. For He deified our nature in Himself by taking it; He could, and did, empty Himself of the visible glory of His Godhead; He could not, by becoming man, cease to be God. He became man, "not by conversion of the Godhead into flesh, but by taking of the Manhood into God." "We worship not a creature," says St. Athanasius[g]; "God forbid! For such an error belongs to heathens and Arians. But we worship the Lord of the creation, the Word of God Incarnate. For although the Flesh, Itself by Itself, is a portion of the things created, yet It became the Body of God. And neither, severing the Body, being such, by Itself apart from the Word, do we worship It; nor, wishing to worship the Word, do we remove Him from the Flesh; but knowing, as I said before, the Scripture, 'The Word was made Flesh,' we own Him, although being in the Flesh, to be God. Who, then, is so senseless as to say to the Lord, 'Remove from the Body that I may worship Thee?' or who so ungodly as, with the frantic Jews, on account of the Body, to say to Him,

---

[e] ag. Arians, i. 8, p. 191, Oxf. Tr. [f] Theodoret on Rom. i. 25.
[g] Ep. ad Adelph. § 3, p. 912, 913, Ben.

'Why dost Thou, being a Man, make Thyself God?' Not such was the leper; for he worshipped the God, being in the Body, and knew that He was God, saying, 'Lord, if Thou wilt, Thou canst make me clean;' and neither, on account of the Flesh, did he account the Word of God a creature; nor, because the Word was the Artificer of all creation, did he make light of the Flesh, wherewith He was arrayed; but he worshipped as in a created temple the Creator of all, and was cleansed. So also the woman with an issue of blood, believing and only touching the hem of His garment, was healed; and the sea, tossing its foam, heard the voice of the Incarnate Word, and ceased its tempest; and the blind from his birth, through the spittle of the Flesh, was healed by the Word; and greater and more marvellous still (for this, perchance, shocked even the most ungodly), when the Lord, being upon the Cross itself, (for the Body was the Lord's, and in It was the Word,) 'the sun was darkened, and the earth shook, the rocks were rent, and the veil of the temple was rent in twain, and many bodies of the saints which slept, arose.'"

The confusion, created by heretics, arose in the ignorance or misbelief of the doctrine of the Incarnation, the fruitful source of manifold heresy. For men, in one or the other way, parted with the belief that our Lord's Divine Nature, being Divine, was unchangeable; that It could not be confused; that It could receive no accession to Itself, so as to be a complement of Itself. For It was all-perfect. When, then, God the Word vouchsafed to take our nature upon Him in the Virgin's womb, He did not unite to Himself a pre-existing nature, so that It should have a distinct personality, but "created that manhood which He took, by taking It, and took It by creating It [h]." His Manhood, real and perfect as It was, was but an adjunct of His Deity. He took our nature, that for us He might suffer, that for us He might die ; that He might bear our sins, that He might offer a full price and ransom for us ; that He might be our High Priest for ever at the Right Hand of God ; yea, that, having redeemed us, He might, by taking a manhood joined to His own Nature, make His Flesh lifegiving, and " through His flesh akin to us might draw up to Him all humanity [i]." " He used it as His instrument for the operation and the shining forth of His Godhead [k]." Yet His Personality is not human but Divine. When, then, we adore Christ, our God, we adore not His Deity and His Humanity separately, but His Deity clothed with His Humanity. This the Church of God proclaimed that she had received from the first, that " God, the Word Incarnate, with His own Flesh was worshipped [l]," rejecting, with anathema, the opposite heresies, that Christ is worshipped in two natures, thus introducing two acts of worship, one appropriated to God the Word, the other appropriated to the Man ; or again, with either destruction of His Humanity, or confusion of the Godhead and Manhood, or the assumption of " one nature from both concurring."

This Divine Nature, then, of our Lord in His Humanity, St. John exhibits as a distinct Object of the praises and thanksgivings of the Church Triumphant. For he saw the beatified beings, whom he was admitted to behold, at times prostrate in adoration before the Lamb, at times as adoring at once Him Who sitteth on the

[h] Hugo de S. Vict., Summa Sent. i. 15. t. iii. p. 431.
[i] Ps. Basil in note k on S. Ath. ag. Arians, p. 444, Oxf. Tr.
[k] S. Ath. ag. Arians, iii. § 53, p. 475, Oxf. Tr.
[l] Conc. Const. ii. can. 9 ; Conc. T. vi. p. 212 Col.

Throne, and the Lamb. At one while, he shews us the four living creatures and four and twenty elders falling down before the Lamb, having, every one of them, harps and golden vials full of incense, which are the prayers of the saints. We hear the new song of redeemed love: "Worthy art Thou ... for Thou wast slain, and hast redeemed us to God by Thy Blood out of every kindred, and tongue, and people, and nation; and hast made us unto our God kings and priests [m]." "Worthy is the Lamb that was slain to receive power, and riches, and wisdom, and strength, and honour, and glory, and blessing [n]." And again, the song is echoed from the whole Church, triumphant, militant, and expectant: "every creature which is in heaven, and on the earth, and under the earth, saying, Blessing, and honour, and glory, and power, be unto Him that sitteth upon the throne, and unto the Lamb for ever and ever [o]." And again, all that great white-robed, palm-bearing "multitude, which no man could number, of all nations, and kindreds, and people, and tongues, stood before the throne, and before the Lamb, saying, with a loud voice, Salvation to our God which sitteth upon the throne, and to the Lamb [p]."

This same, which St. John exhibits in being, as God shewed it him, St. Paul sets forth as the end of the humiliation of the Son of God. God humbled Himself, emptied Himself, to exalt that Manhood which He humbled Himself to take, and then, in Him, all our humanity. In Himself the Son could not be exalted. For He was Co-eternal, Co-equal with God. But He willed to be One Person with the Humanity which He humbled Himself to take. He humbled Himself, so closely to unite Himself with man, that all which could

[m] Rev. v. 8—10.   [n] Ib. 12.   [o] Ib. 13.   [p] Ib. vii. 9, 10.

belong to His Manhood might be spoken of Him as God; what belonged to Him, as God, might be spoken of the Man Christ Jesus. Was it not so? They of old said boldly, "the Passion of Christ my God [q]," "the sufferings of God [r]," "God was dead and buried [s]," because, although God could not suffer or die, He Who for our sakes died and was buried and rose again was Almighty God. "Because of the perfect union of the Flesh which was assumed, and the Godhead which assumed It, the names are interchanged, so that the human is called from the Divine, and the Divine from the Human. Wherefore He Who was crucified was called by Paul 'the Lord of glory;' and He Who is worshipped by all creation, of things in heaven, in earth, and under the earth, is named Jesus [t]." God the Son plainly could not be exalted; for He was in all eternity, "in the form of God." It was the equality with God which He *had*, of which He "held it no desirable thing" to retain the manifestation; but He humbled Himself by "taking upon Him the form of a servant" of God, by "coming to be (by His Birth) in the likeness of man;" (not mere man, being still what He was, Almighty God) "and, being found in guise as a man," [i. e. being, again, not mere man, but personally God, clothed with our humanity,] "He humbled Himself by becoming obedient even unto death, and that the death of the Cross," the shameful, the accursed, the transgressors' doom.

The counterpart of the exaltation relates to the

---

[q] S. Ignat. ad Rom. n. 6. "God suffered;" S. Melito ap. Anast. Hodeg. 12. See St. Ath. ag. Ar., p. 444, n. i.

[r] Tert. de Carn. Christi, c. 5.

[s] Vigil. c. Eutych. ii. 502, ib.; see also Petav. de Inc., ii. 2. 12, 13; iv. 15. 5 sqq.

[t] S. Greg. Nyss. in Apoll., t. iii. 265, 6.

self-same. The humiliation was the veiling of His essential glory, which He had, co-equal with the Father, before the world was, by taking our manhood. The exaltation was of Himself, not in Himself, but in regard to that Manhood which He had taken. *He* was exalted, because the Manhood was exalted which He had made an adjunct of Himself. His Manhood had no separate existence, but was assumed to His own Personality. "His Godhead was in It; the Body was God's^u." "Being God and Man, He was One Christ^v." St. Paul then speaks of Him as being super-eminently exalted by God, because the Manhood was exalted, which was His own. "Wherefore," since He so humbled Himself and was so obedient, "God super-exalted Him, and gave Him that Name,"—that Name which is excellent and glorious above every name,—that saving Name, which was predicted by the angel, which was given beforehand at His Circumcision, which received its full meaning and fulfilment when on the Cross He poured out His Blood, and paid the price of the redemption of the whole world, that "at the name of Jesus every knee should bow, of things in heaven, and things on earth, and things under the earth; and every tongue should confess that Jesus Christ is Lord, to the glory of God the Father." It is, as if he described our worship 1800 years before. All things human have manifoldly changed, are changing. The worship of Jesus, our Lord and God, changes not, being, like Himself, eternal.

And so is fulfilled that solemn prayer of our Lord, "Father, glorify Thou Me with Thyself with that glory which I had with Thee before the world was^x." The

^u St. Ath. ag. Ar., iii. § 31, p. 444, O. T.   ^v Ath. Creed.
^x St. John xvii. 5.

Son never ceased to be in that glory, in that oneness with the Father, in which He eternally is. But as, when on earth, He spoke of Himself, as "the Son of Man Who *is* in heaven [y];" because, as God, He is there and every where eternally; as He said to the Jews, "What and if ye see the Son of Man ascend up where He was before [z]?" although His Divine Person alone, not His Manhood, which was now in one with It, had been there before; as He said, that "the Son of Man hath power on earth to forgive sins [a]," although "none" has that power "but God alone [b]," and the Son of Man had it, only because He was God the Son; as "the Son of Man was Lord of the Sabbath [c]," which "the Lord" God had "blessed and hallowed [d]," because He was One Substance with God Who had so hallowed it; as He saith that the Son of Man shall, in that great day which shall decide eternity, "come in His own glory [e]," although the glory in which He shall come is the glory of the Godhead, since He also calls it "the glory of the Father [f];" as it is said, that in that day "the Son of Man shall send forth *His* angels [g]," although those blessed spirits are "the ministers of God" only, "to do His pleasure [h];" so He, being One Person with God the Son, is glorified with that glory which He had with God before the world was, although then the Manhood existed not.

This worship of "the Word made flesh" began from the moment that He took that Flesh. Elisabeth owned Him as her Lord, ere yet He was born: "Whence is this to me, that the Mother of my Lord should come

---

[y] St. John iii. 13. [z] Ibid. vi. 62. [a] St. Matt. ix. 6.
[b] St. Mark ii. 7.   [c] Ibid. ii. 28. [d] Exod. xx. 11.
[e] St. Matt. xxv. 31. [f] St. Mark viii. 38. [g] St. Matt. xiii. 41.
[h] Ps. ciii. 21.

unto me[1]?" This worship the angels paid Him unseen, when He lay yet in His narrow manger-bed. The shepherds heard their songs of joy, "Glory to God in the Highest, and on earth peace, good will toward men[k];" but, unseen, they worshipped Him, where they told the shepherds that they would find Him; for they obeyed that command, "When He bringeth the First-Begotten into the world, He saith, 'And let all the angels of God worship Him[l].'" This worship they must have paid Him, as He ascended from choir to choir above the highest heavens, as they owned Him the King of Glory. "Lift up your heads, O ye gates; and be ye lift up, ye everlasting doors; and the King of Glory shall come in. Who is the King of Glory? The Lord of Hosts,"—their own Lord, who took this title of "Lord of Hosts" from them,—"He is the King of Glory[m]."

But what on earth? which Prophets had foretold would be His, where kings were to worship Him, where all nations were to serve Him, which He had claimed as His own, but which, as Man, He had left for that "far country[n]," whence He was to return? What on earth? His own Person could not but be, it was, it is, it will be to the end, the centre of the faith, the object of attack, the rock on which His Church should be founded, on which the waves of unbelief would dash themselves; the magnet attracting love and hate, adoration and blasphemy. Had His religion been a philosophy, no need to destroy it: it would have taken its place among the things of earth, and have died. Had it been a mere worship of what men call the Deity (meaning something about as vague

[1] St. Luke i. 43.   [k] Ibid. ii. 14.   [l] Heb. i. 6.
[m] Ps. xxiv. 9, 10.   [n] St. Matt. xxv. 14.

as what the old heathen believed), it would have been admired, have caused no uproar, have been forgotten. But the Jews, and His own "little flock," and the heathen presently, alike understood the issue. Was Jesus what He claimed to be, God? or was He what the Chief Priests and Pharisees called Him to Pilate, "a deceiver?" There was no middle term. Either Almighty God, One Substance with the Father, indwelling in the Father and indwelt by the Father through the absolute numerical Oneness of the Divine Nature, or,—less than man; not such as Socrates or Græcia's wise men, but—it is well to face the alternative, to look it straight, full in the face,—not even an upright man, such as many whom we reverence now on earth, but a deceiver. The Jews sought to extinguish His Name. Either they were Deicides, or He was such as they between whom they had crucified Him, yea, worse than they, by how much spiritual seduction from loyalty to our God and Father, spiritual falsehood, taught in the Name of, and against, the God of Truth, is worse, more desolating, more destructive than sedition of a conquered nation against their temporal masters. And so they forbade to teach in His Name; they gave authority—(it is doubtless, according to the wont of Holy Scripture, but one instance out of many,)—they gave authority to Saul, while "yet breathing out threatenings and slaughter against the disciples of the Lord," to "bind all who should call on the Name of Jesus[o]." To that same Jesus the converted Saul, when struck to the earth by the majesty of His appearing, submitted his whole soul, all which he was, all his life, as to his Lord: "What shall I do, Lord[p]?" To Him he prayed, as washing away his sins,

[o] Acts ix. 1, 14, 21.   [p] Ib. xxii. 10.

when baptized; "calling on the Name of the Lord[q]." To Him he prayed thrice[r] in that distressing temptation which he calls "the thorn in the flesh," that it might depart from him, and received answer, "My grace" (imparted manifestly upon that prayer) "sufficeth for thee," yea, and (it lies in the words) "shall suffice." And should this be an insulated act? What religious act of any religious man is an insulated act? Where we have found help, *there* we again seek it; where it has been opened to us, *there* we again knock; of Him Who has given to us, we again ask. Much more in St. Paul. One word, one act, opens to us a large vision into his inner life. Man's fickleness waves to and fro; stayed and steadfast is the soul whose centre, whose attraction, whose lodestone is Christ! His strength was perfected in this one weakness; His might, upon St. Paul's prayer, resided upon him as its home. What, then, of those other weaknesses in which his soul rested content, in which to be weak was to be mighty? He whose life was the life of Christ in him[s]; he, in whom what he wrought, Christ wrought[t]; he, in whose body Christ was evermore magnified[u]; he, who could do all things in Christ instrengthening him[x]; he, in whose heart Christ dwelt, and by whose mouth Christ spake; in whom Christ was. Whence could he have this closest union and communion with Christ, but that that intense prayer in his weakness, which he mentions the rather because it was answered otherwise than he asked it, was but one flash which shines forth from his God-illumined soul?

St. Paul prayed not only to Jesus but in that cor-

[q] Acts xxii. 16.   [r] 2 Cor. xii. 8.   [s] Gal. ii. 20.
[t] Rom. xv. 18.   [u] Phil. i. 20.
[x] Ib iv. 13. See further in Dr. Heurtley's "Prayer to Christ," p. 15.

responding act, wherein we are so mean and niggard towards Almighty God, he thanks alike God and Jesus. He thanks Jesus as his Lord for that Divine act of grace which was the turning-point of his whole life: "I thank Christ Jesus our Lord Who instrengthened me, that He accounted me faithful, putting me into the ministry, being a blasphemer and persecutor and insulter ʸ."

And what of others? What were his manifold benedictions but prayers to his Lord and God, Christ Jesus, either by Himself or with God the Father ᶻ with Whom the Son is One, that He, Jesus, would be present with the spirit of those whom He blessed; that Jesus would, equally with the Father, pour peace, love, faith, grace, mercy into their souls; that He would comfort their hearts and stablish them in every good word and work? St. Paul gathers into one thought the whole body of Christians, as, "all who call upon the Name of" our common "Lord, Jesus Christ ᵃ;" he speaks of all who were Christ's disciples in sincerity and truth, as those who "call on the Lord with a pure heart ᵇ." Devotion and prayer to Jesus was the characteristic of Christians. He, One and the same Lord of all, was ever-abounding in wealth toward all who call upon Him, gushing forth in one ever-flowing munificence of grace and love to all everywhere who looked to Him for aid; not of any temporary, fleeting graces, but of "grace upon grace," grace heaped upon grace, grace issuing in salvation. For so had the prophet foretold, "Whosoever shall call upon the Name of the Lord ᶜ" (i.e. as is plain from the context ᵈ, the Lord Jesus,) "shall be saved."

ʸ 1 Tim. i. 12.   ᶻ 1 Cor. i. 3.   ᵃ Ib. ver. 2.
ᵇ 2 Tim. ii. 22.   ᶜ Rom. x. 13; Joel ii. 32.
ᵈ For it continues, "How shall they call upon Him, in Whom they have not believed?" See Alford, *ad loc.*

Momentary prayer obtains the grace it asks for; abiding prayer obtains abiding grace; prayer for perseverance obtains the grace of perseverance; prayer, persevering to the end, obtains grace in the end; grace in the end yields the soul to salvation.

What one of the glorious company of the Apostles did, in so central a point of Christian faith, self-evidently all must have done. To Jesus, probably, St. Peter addressed that prayer about the choice to Judas' vacated place: "Lord, discerner of the heart of all[e]." To Jesus, in that most perfect imitation of His close of His earthly life, in entire resignation and Divine love, St. Stephen yielded his soul in His own prayers as Man, "Lord Jesus, receive my spirit;" "Lord, lay not this sin to their charge[f]." How did he, whom Jesus loved, fall unreproved at *His* Feet[g], on Whose breast he once lay, ascribing to Him the incommunicable "glory and might[h]," which belong to God only! How does he thank Him for His ever-abiding, ever-present love[i], and for that more than atoning, more than forgiving act; that act, in one, atoning, forgiving, re-creating, sanctifying; "Who loveth us, and washed us from our sins in His own Blood[k]!" How does he pray for grace and peace, to issue to the Churches, at once from the Eternal God, and from Him in Whom the Godhead was enshrined, with Whom It was united by that hypostatic union, which was closer, more inter-penetrating, than any union, save of the Persons of the self-inexisting Trinity in Unity!

And since the Father and the Son are One, and our Lord had said, as meaning one and the same thing,

---

[e] Acts i. 24.   [f] Ib. vii. 59, 61.   [g] Rev. i. 17.
[h] Ib. 6; comp. 1 Tim. vi. 16; Heb. xiii. 21; 1 Pet. iv. 11, v. 11.
[i] ἀγαπῶντι.   [k] Rev. i. 4, 5.

"Whatsoever ye shall ask of the Father in My Name, He may give it you[1]," and "Whatsoever ye shall ask in My Name, that will I do[m];" so St. John, summing up the end and object of his own teaching, "that ye may know that ye have eternal life, and that ye may believe in the name of the Son of God[n]," adds, as to Him of Whom he had so spoken, "and this is the confidence which we have towards Him, that if we ask anything according to His Will, He heareth us. And if we know that He heareth us whatsoever we ask, we know that we have the petitions which we have asked from Him." What a volume of accumulated prayer, asked of and granted by the Son of God! "We know that whatsoever we have asked for, that"—not we *had* simply, but, "we *have*," an ever-present possession of all we ever asked Him.

Ere yet St. John had left the earth, the heathen Pliny knew of the Christian worship that, "in meetings before day-break, they sang responsively a hymn to Christ as God[o]." "Very many Psalms and songs of the brethren," we are early told [p], "written from the beginning by the faithful, hymn Christ, the Word of God, entitling Him God." The heretic, Paul of Samosata, in order to make way for his heresy of the simple humanity of Christ, had to do away with those Psalms to our Lord Jesus Christ, feigning that they were recent [q]. Morning by morning they echoed those lauds in Heaven: "Glory to God in the highest [r]." They prayed, as we still

---

[1] St. John xv. 16.   [m] Ib. xiv. 13.   [n] 1 Ep. v. 13—15.
[o] Plin. Ep. x. 97.   [p] Caius, A.D. 210, in Eus. H. E. v. 28.
[q] Ep. Conc. Antioch. in Eus. H. E. vii. 30.
[r] The beginning of the hymn is given in the ancient *de virginitate*, in St. Athan. Works, and by St. Chrysostom, Hom. 68 in St. Matt., as a morning hymn; the whole, with variations, in the Apost. Const. vii. 47. See further Abp. Ussher, who thinks that it is one of the early hymns men-

carry on their prayer: "O Lord God, Lamb of God, Son of the Father, Who takest away the sins of the world, have mercy upon us;" and the rest of that prayer, which, in deepest thankfulness, you have said so often to Him, blessing Him, that He Alone is holy, He Alone is the Lord, He, Jesus Christ, "with the Holy Ghost in the glory of God the Father." Evening by evening, as they came to the setting sun, they hymned Father, Son, and Holy Ghost, and Him, through Whom we approach to God, God and Man: "Worthy art Thou to be hymned at all times with holy voices, Son of God, Who givest life; wherefore the world glorifieth Thee^s."

"The world glorifieth Thee!" Ere the second century had expired, Tertullian, enumerating the narrow bounds of those world-empires which had passed away, appeals to the Jews: "Why speak I of the Romans, who guard their empire by the outposts of their legions, nor can stretch the might of their reign beyond those nations? But the reign and Name of Christ is stretched forth everywhere; everywhere He is believed; by all those nations He is worshipped; everywhere He reigns; everywhere He is adored; He is given equally to all everywhere; kings stand in no greater favour with Him; no barbarian hath an inferior joy; no dignities or birth confer distinct merits; to all, He is the same; to all, the King; to all, the Judge; to all, Lord and God^t."

This seemed to the Heathen "madness", that, after the immutable, everlasting God, Parent of all, they alleged, that Christians gave the second place to

---

tioned by the writer in Eusebius (see p. 87) *De Symbolis*, n. 3, Works, vii. 335, 6.

^s See in Routh, *Rel. S.* iii. 515. St. Basil (*de Sp. S.* c. 29,) speaks of it as "ancient," of its "evidence, from its antiquity."

^t Adv. Jud. i. 7, p. 213, Rig.   ^u St. Justin, Apol i. 13, p. 9, Oxf. Tr.

a Man, Who had been crucified;" "they worshipped exceedingly One Who had lately appeared[x];" "the Son of Man, under the plea that He was the Great God[y];" "the leader of their sedition, Whom they called the Son of God[z]." "That great Man, Who was crucified in Palestine because He brought into the world this new religion[a]."

And the Apologists answered the Jews that so had their own Prophets foretold in express terms (as they did), that Christ should both suffer, and be worshipped, and be God; nay, they say that the Jews admitted this[b], only that they dared to deny that Jesus was the Christ. They worshipped One, (they said,) not Man only but God. "We worship," they said[c], "One God, the Father and the Son, and do not give an excess of worship to Him Who appeared of late as though, before, He were not. For we believe Himself Who said, 'Before Abraham was, I am[d].'" They told the Heathen that what these counted madness, they with reason did, "having learned that He, Who was born Jesus Christ, Who was crucified under Pontius Pilate,

---

[x] Celsus in Origen, c. Cels. viii. 12.   [y] Ib. 15.   [z] Ib. 14.

[a] Lucian de morte Peregrini, t. i. p. 565, Gr. "I come now to the Passion itself, which is wont to be objected to us as a reproach, that we both worship a Man and One who was by men afflicted by a notable punishment and excruciated." Lact. iv. 16. "'But,' one saith, 'the gods are not therefore your enemies, because you worship God Almighty, but because you both believe that one, born man, and (what is infamous to vile persons) put to death by the punishment of the cross, still survives, and you adore Him with daily supplications.'" Arnob. i. 36, "A man, punished capitally for guilt, and the cross's sad wood, they relate, are their worships, fitting altars for lost and guilty men, that they should worship what they deserve." Cæcil. in Minut. Fel. p. 86, Ouz., "We worship the gods with joy, feastings, songs, plays, revellings, and wantonness; but you a crucified man, Whom they cannot please who enjoy all these things." Heathen judge to St. Epipodius; Ruinart, Act. Mart., p. 64.

[b] St. Justin, Dial. c. Tryph. n. 68, p. 160, Oxf. Tr.

[c] Orig. c. Cels. viii. 17.   [d] St. John viii. 58.

was the Son of the true God[e]." "We are no worshippers of insensate stones, but of the Only God, before all and above all, and of His Christ, being indeed God the Word before all ages[f]." To this they exhort them: "Believe, O man, in Him, Who is Man and God. Believe, O man, in the Living God, Who suffered and is worshipped[g]."

This was the confession of the Martyrs.

"The common people knoweth Christ as one among men, whence one might the rather suppose us worshippers of a man. We say openly and, while ye torture us, mangled and gory we cry out, We worship God through Christ: believe Him a Man; it is in Him and through Him that God willeth to be known and worshipped[h]."

To Him they cried, when their tortures were passed human endurance. We still have their broken words faithfully preserved. To Him they looked for aid, for Whom they suffered; yea, Who in them was persecuted, and suffered. To Him they prayed: "Christ, I pray, have mercy; Son of God, help[i]." "Christ, my Lord, let me not be confounded." "I pray, O Christ, give endurance. Thou art the hope of Life[k]."

[e] St. Justin, Apol. i. 13. p. 5.
[f] St. Melito, Apol. in Chron. Pasch., p. 259; Gall. i. 678.
[g] St. Clem. Coh. c. 10, p. 30. Sylb.
[h] Tert. Apol. n. 21, p. 50, Oxf. Tr. Maximian afterwards "commands that the *worshippers of Christ* [Christicolas], unless they would sacrifice to idols, should perish by exquisite deaths." Pass. St. Victor, &c., Ruinart, p. 301.
[i] Saturninus, Acta Mart. in Baron. A. 303. n. 48.
[k] Thus Dativus, Ib. n. 44, "So, while he is wholly in Christ and, now worn out, invokes Him with his last words, he breathes out his blessed spirit." Alexander, in Act. Epipod. et Alex, n. 11; Ruin., p. 66. Saturninus Jun., Ib. n. 54., "O Lord Jesus Christ, Hope of the hopeless, grant me to finish my course, and to offer the shedding of my blood for a sacrifice and libation, for all their sakes who are afflicted for Thee." St. Theodotus in Ruinart., p. 364.

Him they confessed before their judges, as the object of their adoration: "I am the servant of Christ; Him I confess with my mouth, hold in my heart, adore unceasingly[1]." "There is no king beside Him Whom I have seen[m]; and I adore and worship Him; and if for His worship I die a thousand deaths, His will I be, as I have begun. Christ from my mouth, Christ from my heart, tortures cannot take[n]." "The sacrifice of prayer and deprecation, of compunction and praise, I must offer to the Living and True God, to the King of all ages, Christ[o]." To Him they offered themselves as a living sacrifice: "Father, Son, and Holy Ghost I adore; the Holy Trinity I adore; beside whom there is no God. I am a Christian. I sacrifice myself to Christ God[p]."

[1] Alexander in Acta St. Felic. n. 3. in Ruinart, Acta Mart., p. 22. "Christ, with the Father and the Holy Spirit, I confess to be God; and it is meet that I give back my soul to Him Who is both my Creator and Redeemer." Acta St. Epipod. Ruin., p. 65.

[m] In a vision. Ib.

[n] Acta St. Genesii ex mimo Martyris; Ruinart, p. 284. *Q.* "What God do you worship?" *Polemon.* "Christ." *Q.* "What, then, is He another?" *Pol.* "No, but the same, Whom those, too, confessed a little before." Acta St. Pionii, n. 9, about A.D. 250, Ruin., p. 129. "What God do ye worship?" *Pionius.* "Him Who made heaven," &c. *Q.* "Sayest thou Him Who was crucified?" *Pion.* "I say, Him Whom the Father sent for the salvation of the world." Ib., n. 16, p. 134. "We render honour to Cæsar; fear and worship we yield to Christ, the true God." St. Donata in Act. Mart. Scillit. A.D. 200; Ruinart, p. 80.

[o] Act. SS. Martr. Petri, Andreæ, &c.; Ruinart, p. 147.

[p] *Consular.* "Cease, Euplius, from this madness. Adore the Gods, and thou shalt be free." *Euplius.* "I adore Christ, I detest dæmons. Do what thou wilt, I am a Christian."—*C.* "Unhappy one, adore the gods, Mars, Apollo, Æsculapius." *E.* "Father, and Son, and Holy Spirit I adore; the Holy Trinity I adore; besides Which there is no God."—*C.* "Sacrifice, if thou wouldest be freed." *E.* "Now I sacrifice myself to Christ, God. I can do no more. In vain thou essayest; I am a Christian." Acta Euplii, n. 2; Ruinart, p. 440. "I never sacrificed, nor sacrifice, save to the One God, and our Lord Jesus Christ His Son, Who was born and suffered." Acta St. Crispini, Ruin., p. 494. "We sacrifice to our Lord Jesus Christ," &c. Acta St. Mammarii in Mabillon, Analect. t. iv. ap. Ruinart, p. 367, n. 2; add Acta Mart. Lugd., n. 14; Ruin., p. 56.

"Lord God of heaven and earth,—Jesu Christ, to Thee I bend my neck as a victim, Who abidest for ever, to Whom is glory and majesty for all ages[q]." In thanksgiving to Him, their God, they closed their lives: "Us Christ governeth, Who hath brought us to this glory. Glory to Thee, O Christ, Who hast vouchsafed to gather us with the holy Martyrs[r]." "Thanks be to Thee, O Christ; keep me, who suffer these things for Thee.—I adore Christ[s]." "The eternal kingdom, the undefiled kingdom dawneth, O Lord Jesu Christ. We are Christians. We serve Thee. Thou art our Hope; Thou art the hope of Christians. O God most Holy, O God most High, O God Almighty, we give Thee praise for Thy Name[t]."

Such, then, was the Will of the Eternal Trinity towards us, Father, Son, and Holy Ghost, not only that we should be admitted to the blissful adoration and intuition of the Triune God, through the Incarnation and Atoning Death of God the Son, but that He Himself, our Redeeming Lord and God, should, in His Humanity, be a distinct Object of our contemplation and adoration and thanksgiving and joy. One indeed is God, and the

---

[q] Acta St. Felic. in Baron. A. 302, n. 123; add Acta St. Afræ in Ruinart, p. 502.

[r] Acta Olympii in Baron., A.D. 259, n. 30. "Bl. Crispina said, 'I give thanks to [my God, and my] Christ. I bless the Lord, Who has vouchsafed thus to deliver me from thy hands.'" Acta St. Crispinæ, Ruin., p. 496.

[s] Acta Euplii, Ruinart, p. 439; add Acta Mart. Scillit. fin. Ruin., p. 78. Act. Lucian. et Marcian., n. 7; Ib., p. 154. Acta St. Afræ, n. 3; Ib. 502. Acta St. Irenæi, n. 5, p. 434; Acta St. Philippi, n. 10; Ib., p. 450. Acta Probi, Ib. 481. St. Ampelii, Baron. A 303, n. 52; St. Felic. Baron, l. c. Acta St. Ignatii; Ruinart, pp. 12, 698: "I give Thee thanks, O Lord, because Thou hast vouchsafed to honour me with perfect love, to be with Thy Apostle Paul placed in iron chains." Ep. Eccl. Smyrn. de Mart. St. Polycarp n. 14. Cotel. Patr. Ap. ii. 199.

[t] Acta Theliæ in Baron 1 c. A.D. 303, n. 41.

God-enabled eye of the blessed shall see the truth which our Lord enounced: "I am in the Father, and the Father in Me [u]." They, being empowered to see the Essence of God, must see, how "the Holy Ghost reposes and habitates in God [x]," how "All the Father embosometh the Son [y]," and how "the Father is the natural Place of the Son [z]." The Father has in Him the Son; and, again, He is in the Son, because of the identity of the Substance. "Each is contemplated, and is truly in the Other [a]." "The Union is not as that of our Lord's Godhead and Humanity (intimate as was the blending of Both in the One Person of our Lord), but as the whole Power, Life, Substance, Wisdom, Essence of the Father is the very Essence, Substance, Wisdom, Life, and Power of the Son [b]." So that he who sees the Essence of the Son, or the Son as He Is, must needs see the Essence of the Father and of the Holy Ghost. For they are One. And he who adores God the Father must needs, by one act, adore the Son and the Holy Ghost, since the Holy Ghost is "co-glorified and co-worshipped with the Father and the Son;" and the Trinity is worshipped in the Unity, which It is, and the Unity in the Trinity, which co-exist and in-exist as One.

Yet *there*, too, we must retain a separate love and thankfulness for that which in their Oneness of Being Each separate Person has done for us. For although

---

[u] St. John xiv. 10.

[x] St. Dionys. Rom. in St. Ath. ag. Arian., p. 46, Oxf. Tr.

[y] An orthodox expression in the Macrostich, Ib. p. 116, the correlative of St. John i. 18: "The only-begotten Son, Who is in the bosom of the Father."

[z] St. Cyril, Thes. vii. t. v. p. 5, quoted in St. Ath. ag. Ar., p. 399, n. a. "The Son is the place of the Father, as the Father, too, is the place of the Son." St. Jerome in Ezek. iii. 12. Ib.

[a] St. Cyril de Trin. vi. p. 621; Ib. p. 403, n. i.

[b] Thomassin de Trin. 28, 1. Ib.

inseparable are the works of the Trinity, and the Father so loved the world that He sent His Only-Begotten Son to die for us; yea, and according to His Sacred Humanity that is true, that "the Lord God and His Spirit sent [e]" Him, yet it was One of the All-Holy Trinity Who vouchsafed to take our nature upon Him, and, in it, unsuffering to suffer for us through that Flesh which He took. Why does the heart so throb at the Name of Jesus? Why is it so jubilant? Why so instrengthening? Why does it so melt us, if we are dry? Why does it so kindle us, if we are cold? Why does it diffuse in us such serenity, if we are sad? Why, if we are half-dead, does it give us life? Why, if we sit in darkness, does it flash light into our souls? Why, if we are quivering in temptation, does it give us strength? Why, if we are terrified at our past sins, does a ray burst forth from it, which transmutes the dark cloud into the crimson tinge of His Blood? Why, but because it is the "Name Which is above every name;" because the Name of Redeemer is in one way mightier than that of Creator, (for it cost more to redeem our souls than to create them,) because it is the Name of God, for us and for our salvation, become Man.

Every thing good and Divine on earth is a counterpart of something more wondrously beautiful or visibly Divine in Heaven. We cannot think of Jesus here but with adoring love, or loving adoration. We must cease to believe in Him, ere we could cease to adore Him. But Jesus cannot cease to be. Nay, rather, we are told that when God shall be all in all [d], and all shall be subdued unto Him, and the whole multitude of His elect shall be perfected, and Christ, i.e. Whole Christ, Himself in His Human Nature our Head, and we His,

[e] Isa. xlviii. 16.   [d] 1 Cor. xv. 28.

as yet, imperfect members, shall be subject to God through the entire subjection of His whole redeemed Body in their whole compass and their entire selves to the mind of God [e],—then, too, His kingdom shall have no end [f]; then, too, more than before, " shall every knee bow in the Name of the Lord Jesus, and every tongue confess that Jesus Christ is Lord, to the glory of God the Father [g];" then, too, the Humanity of Christ, and God manifest in that Human Form, will be a distinct joy and adoration in Heaven. For then, too, that "river of living water [h]," that torrent of pleasure, that unceasing effluence of beatitude, that overstreaming fulness of joy which shall, with its multitudinous bliss, inundate the souls, and minds, and senses of the beatified, shall issue forth from the one throne of God and of the Lamb. There, amid all the varied fruition in that blissful Paradise of God, where all curse is done away for ever, the central joy is, that the one Throne of God and of the Lamb shall be in it [i]; and St. John speaks as though we should see Them with one vision, and adore Them with one adoration, and bear the Name of God and of Jesus, as One Name, upon our foreheads. For, having spoken of the Throne of God and of the Lamb therein, he adds, "And His servants shall worship *Him*, and shall see *His* Face; and *His* Name shall be on their foreheads." And again, "The Lord God Almighty is the temple thereof, and the Lamb [k]." There shall be no visible temple, for God shall, if we attain, be our place. In Him we shall see Himself; in Him we shall contemplate, adore, praise, thank, bless Himself. Yet then, too, we shall be in

[e] See Fathers in Petav. de Trin., iii. 5 ; de Incarn., xii 18, 13.
[f] St. Luke i. 33. [g] Phil. ii. 10, 11.
[h] Rev. xxii. 1. [i] Rev. xxii. 3, 4. [k] Ibid. 23.

Christ; for not God only, but the Lamb also, shall be our temple. "And the glory of God shall enlighten" that city of the blessed; His uncreated glory filling it with the beatific, illumining, transporting light of His Godhead; and yet then, too, undimmed by that essential Light, shall shine out the glory of the Humanity of Jesus; undimmed by It, because, although seen distinctly, It is the self same, "The glory," Jesus says, "Which I had with Thee, before the world was[1]." It shall shine with a separate, transporting lustre, an illumining, beatifying beauty. For so God says, "The glory of God did lighten it, and the Lamb is the Light thereof." We could not even imagine it otherwise. Heaven would not be a Christian's heaven without Jesus. No, even in this land of shadows, amid the necessary distractions of this life's duties, amidst our infirmities, whether self-contracted or incidental to our wayfaring condition, it would be misery to think that our poor praises and thanksgivings here for His redeeming love would be all; that we should not endlessly love and praise Him for that mercy which itself "endureth for ever." Our thanklessness is well-nigh intolerable to our better selves now. But to think that we should never see Him, to praise and adore Him,—not worthily of Himself, for *that* were impossible to created love (His Blessed Mother, by reason of her creatureship, could not adequately praise Him), but—to the utmost of our created capacity, it would leave (which is impossible) an unfilled blank, an unsatisfied longing, in Heaven. It is our joy and consolation now to think of that great white Throne, and, in faith, to behold Him there; to see those Eyes, which once wept over Jerusalem, now beaming not only with the human

St. John xvii. 5.

love of God-Man, but with the Infinite Love of His Godhead; to behold those Hands, once stretched forth to heal, once nailed on the Cross; or those Sacred Feet, which went up and down to save the lost, and which we, with Magdalene, would so long to dare to touch, and (if it could but be) to kiss with penitent love; or, even chiefly, that wounded Side, riven, that we might hide ourselves therein, pouring forth from those Wounds which for us He received, not His Redeeming Blood as once, but the radiant Majesty of His Divine love, lighting and love-enkindling the utmost bounds of God's creation, wherever there is a being which can love. Our consolation and joy is to know that, wherever our place be, although the last and lowest, *there* too we shall "ever be with the Lord[m];" there we shall speak to Him, adore Him, love Him, as our own Jesus; "My Lord and my God[n]." "O, it is good for us to be here[o]." Would that we could, in thought at least, be thus with Him in the holy mount! Would that we could ever bear about with us the dying of the Lord Jesus, that He could be our life, as He is invisibly our life's Source!

But there is an awful gulf, an awful Day, an awful aspect of our Divine (would we may say our Dear) Lord, between; the gulf of death, the Day of Judgment, the truth that "we believe that Thou shalt come to be our Judge." Yet He Who shall be our Judge is Omnipotent to save. He has "the keys of death and hell;" He, not Satan, its prince and our accuser; He shall be our Judge, Who died that we might not die the second death; Who liveth that we might also live through Him, in Him, to Him, with Him; through Him, by His redemption; in Him, by His Sacraments and His

---

[m] 1 Thess. iv. 17.   [n] St. John xx. 28.   [o] St. Mark ix. 5.

Spirit; to Him, in our lives, by His grace; with Him, in eternity, to adore and to love Him.

Only now, in the day of salvation; now, in this season of penitence; now, while the door is not shut to; now, when He anew calleth thee, turn to Him, if thou hast not yet turned; resolve, by His grace, to break off any deadly sin if thou yet be in one; if not, pray for true, abiding, loving sorrow, that thou didst ever displease Him; pray, day by day, for that His great gift—perseverance against that sin, perseverance unto the end; remember, whenever thou canst, His poor, (and now, those penitent sinners who, with thee, have been snatched from the jaws of hell [p]). Pray Him, with the penitent Robber, "Lord, remember me when Thou comest in Thy kingdom; though last, least, lowest, Lord, remember me;" and He Who came, not to destroy men's lives but to save them, will in that dread Day remember thee, deliver thee, that thou too mayest for ever behold His Face, for ever have the beatitude of adoring Him, of loving Him, of being loved by Him.

[p] There was a collection for a Penitentiary.

SERMON VI.

The Victor, on His Throne, the Mediator between God and Man.

HEBREWS vii. 25.

"Wherefore He is able also to save them to the uttermost that come unto God by Him, seeing He ever liveth to make intercession for them."

THE subject to which I have to invite your attention this evening is,—"The Victor, on His Throne, the Mediator between God and Man."

You have had already brought before you, in this course of Lenten Sermons, the various stages which Holy Scripture unfolds in the gradual development of the great scheme of redemption through the only-begotten Son of God. Your thoughts have been carried back to a point beyond the limits of time, when in the "*Counsels of Eternity*" He was "foreordained before the foundation of the world," as the Redeemer of our race: you have reviewed the "*Times of Preparation*"—those long ages of preliminary education and training—which God, in His infinite Wisdom, saw fit to interpose between the Fall and the Restoration, between the first dim promise of a Redeemer and the actual advent of the "Desire of all Nations." You have contemplated "the great mystery of godliness, *God manifest in the flesh;*" when He, who was "the brightness of His Father's glory and the express image of His person," emptied Himself of His Divine majesty and glory, and "took upon Him the form of a servant, and was made in the likeness of men;" "for us men, and for our salvation, came down from heaven, was incarnate by the Holy Ghost of the Virgin Mary, and was made man." You have beheld Him, after being "made a little lower than the angels, for the suffering of death," "*exalted to His Throne*" on the right hand of the Majesty in the heavens. Seated there on His mediatorial throne, you have regarded Him as "*the Object of Divine Worship,*" the centre of countless multitudes of the host of heaven, uttering, as with the voice of many waters, their hymn of adoration, "Worthy is the Lamb that was slain to receive power, and riches, and wisdom, and strength, and honour, and glory, and blessing;"—a strain taken up and re-echoed by every creature in heaven and earth, "Blessing, and honour, and glory, and power be unto Him that sitteth upon the throne, and unto the Lamb for ever and ever."

With minds thus prepared, you come to the contemplation of the subject proposed for our special consideration this evening,—"The Victor, on His Throne, the Mediator between God and Man."

This introduces us to the all-important subject of the *Priesthood* of the Lord Jesus Christ. I need not remind you that, among the topics of which the Apostle Paul treats most largely and elaborately in the Epistle to the Hebrews, the subject of the High-Priesthood of Christ holds a conspicuous place. The Jew, accustomed to the gorgeous temple-worship at Jerusalem, would naturally deem it an essential defect in the Christian system, that it had no proper ritual or ceremonial worship, and, especially, no priesthood, through whose ministry and sacrificial mediation God might be approached and propitiated. We know how the same craving after a sacerdotal religion corrupted Christianity in later ages, until, at length, it became, in this respect, little better than a modified Judaism. St. Paul addresses himself with especial care to answer this alleged deficiency in the Gospel scheme. He shews that every important end which the Jewish sacrificial system could accomplish was secured by Christianity, and in a much higher and more perfect manner; inasmuch as the incarnate Son of God *Himself* discharged the mediatorial functions of the Levitical High-Priest, and in His own person supplied the place of the abolished sacrifices of the Mosaic Law.

Now, the priestly office of Christ embraces two distinct, though closely related, functions: namely, first, that of *Atonement*, or satisfaction for sin; and, secondly, that of *Intercession*, founded upon the Atonement. The former of these functions — that of Atonement — our Blessed Lord discharged ONCE FOR ALL, by His vicarious sufferings and death upon the Cross, and by His oblation of Himself in heaven, the true Holy of Holies, of which the earthly sanctuary was only the image and shadow. The vicarious sacrifice which took place upon earth, and the oblation of it which was made in heaven, after the Ascension, constitute two intimately connected parts of the same expiatory action, which was typified in the Jewish ritual by the high-priest's slaying the victim, on the great day of atonement, outside the sanctuary, and then presenting the blood before the mercy-seat in the Holy of Holies. This whole expiatory action—the sacrifice on earth, the oblation in heaven

—took place once for all, and was never more to be repeated:—"Not by the blood of goats and calves, but by His own Blood, He entered in once into the holy place, having obtained eternal redemption for us."

The second function belonging to Christ's priestly office—that of Intercession—He perpetually exercises, at the right hand of God, and will continue to exercise until the close of His mediatorial kingdom. This perpetual Intercession which He carries on in heaven is based upon, and derives its efficacy from, the Atonement made and perfected once for all.

I shall presently inquire a little more particularly in what this intercession consists. As a preliminary step, it is important to bear in mind that, in several passages of the Apostolic epistles, and especially in the epistle now before us, this function of intercession, while it is based on that of expiation or atonement, is yet very carefully and clearly discriminated from it. In the eighth chapter of Romans, for example, we have a *locus classicus* on the subject:—"who is he that condemneth? It is Christ that died" (made atonement once for all for sin by His death on the Cross), "yea rather, that is risen again, who is even at the right hand of God, who also maketh intercession"—(ἐντυγχάνει, *continues* to make intercession)—"for us."

But it is in the Epistle to the Hebrews that we find these two functions, or aspects, of Christ's priesthood most clearly distinguished. Thus, at the close of the second chapter we read, "Wherefore in all things it behoved Him to be made like unto His brethren, that He might be a merciful and faithful High-Priest in things pertaining to God, to make reconciliation for the sins of the people;"—this is the first part of His sacerdotal office: the second is stated in the following verse, "For in that He Himself hath suffered being tempted, He is able to succour them that are tempted;" or, as it is more fully declared in the fourth chapter, "we have not an high-priest which cannot be touched with the feeling of our infirmities; but was in all points tempted like as we are, yet without sin. Let us therefore come boldly to the throne of grace, that we may obtain mercy, and find grace to help in time of need." The union of the human and divine natures in the person of our Redeemer—*Jesus, the Son of God,*—rendered His atonement of surpassing value, made Him a great High-Priest; His human nature renders Him a merciful and sympathizing Intercessor and Advocate at the throne of grace. Again, in the chapter now before us, we have the intercessional and sacrificial aspects of Christ's priesthood most explicitly discriminated in the twenty-fourth and following verses:—"But He (Jesus), because He continueth ever, hath His priesthood unchangeable. Wherefore He is able also to save to the uttermost" (that is to say, not only in this world but in the next) "them who come unto God by Him, seeing He ever liveth to make intercession for them." . . . "who needeth not daily, as those high-priests, to offer up sacrifice, first for His own sins, and then for the people's: for this He did once, when He offered up Himself." I will add but one passage more—the very remarkable one in the ninth chapter, where we read (twenty-fourth and two following verses), "For Christ did not enter into holy places made with hands, which are figures of the true, but into heaven itself, now to appear in the presence of God for us"—to manifest Himself, face to face with God, on our behalf, as our Advocate and Intercessor; not like the Jewish high-priest, who dared not look on the mercy-seat except through the cloud of incense interposed between him and it:—"Nor yet," continues the Apostle, "that He should offer (sacrificially offer up) Himself often, as the high-priest entereth into the holy place every year with blood of others; ... but now once, in the end of the world, hath He appeared to put away sin by the sacrifice of Himself."

The importance of keeping steadily in view the distinction, so clearly marked in Scripture, between these two functions of Christ's priestly office—the expiatory sacrifice and oblation offered once for all, and the perpetual intercession, based upon that sacrifice, which He is ever making at God's right hand—the importance of insisting on this distinction, I say, appears from the fact that two opposite, and in some respects equally dangerous, errors have arisen from not sufficiently observing it. Socinus and his followers, relying on some passages in this Epistle to the Hebrews which they have misunderstood or misrepresented, have contended that the offering of Christ, by which our sins are said to be expiated, was not perfected on the Cross, and by the shedding of His blood there, but is still going on in heaven, and by the presentation of Himself before God on our behalf. They maintain that Christ is perpetually expiating our sins, and that this expiation consists merely in His constantly *interceding* for us; by which intervention He averts in some way or another (*quodammodo*) the wrath of God from us, and saves us, not from the guilt of our sins, but from the punishment due to them. In fact, Christ's atonement, in any proper sense of the word, is denied; and His intercession, which is really the consequence and effect of His atonement, is substituted in its place.

The Church of Rome, on the other hand, obliterates,

or at least obscures, the distinction between Christ's atonement and His intercession, by virtually resolving the latter into the former. She also maintains that the expiatory sacrifice of Christ was not offered once for all upon the Cross, but is being perpetually offered, in heaven by our Lord Himself, and on earth by His priests in the sacrifice of the Mass: and that, by means of the perpetual repetition of this expiatory sacrifice, pardon is procured for the sins of the living and the dead, mercy obtained, and grace communicated. The mediation or intercession of Christ at the right hand of God is, in fact, neither more nor less than a continuation, or perpetual representation, of the sacrifice made upon the Cross. In order to evade the force of the passages in which the one sacrifice of Christ, once for all offered, is so plainly and emphatically asserted, the scholastic fiction has been adopted, which distinguishes between the one bloody sacrifice on the Cross, and the perpetual unbloody repetition of it in the Mass.

Nor is it merely with respect to the sacrifice of the Mass that this virtual identification of the Atonement and the Intercession of the Lord Jesus Christ has produced evil results. It is also the direct source of one of the greatest practical corruptions which Christianity has ever undergone. When once the mediation of our Lord upon His throne in heaven was made to consist in the perpetual representation or reproduction of His sacrifice, His office of Intercessor was lost sight of and systematically suppressed. And when men ceased to be taught that we have a great High-Priest who can Himself be touched with the feeling of our infirmities, and who, in virtue of the sympathy arising from an actual experience of all our sorrows and sinless infirmities, ever liveth Himself to make intercession for us,—when men ceased to be taught this, they very naturally looked out for a class of mediators, with human sympathies like their own, by propitiating whom they hoped to have their petitions favourably received at the throne of grace. Their wishes in this respect were soon met, or, rather, were already anticipated, by their spiritual guides, whose interest it was to foster and minister to cravings of this kind. These intermediate intercessors have, as might be expected, intercepted the devotion and worship due to the great Intercessor Himself. The more exalted the saint, and the more tender, at the same time, the sympathy supposed to be felt for the suppliant, the more intense, of course, became the devotion, the more profound the homage. And hence, by a very natural, though not less fearful, process of development, a fourth person (with reverence be it said) has been virtually added to the Godhead, and a created, sinful being— "highly favoured," indeed, but still a *creature* like ourselves—has been elevated to a rank, confessedly all but equal, virtually superior, in dignity and honour, to that of the Son of God Himself! Such has been the practical effect of ignoring or explaining away the fundamental truth that, in heaven, as well as upon earth, there is but "one Mediator between God and men, the man Christ Jesus," and that "through Him (and Him alone) we have access by one Spirit unto the Father."

Let us now briefly consider what our blessed Lord does for us, as the Victor on His throne.

Our text says that "He ever liveth to make intercession for those who approach unto God through Him"—through faith, that is, in His person and His atoning work. This intercession, so far as we can gather directly or by inference from Scripture, appears to include several particulars. The first and most important aspect of it is this, that our great High-Priest continually pleads before God the merits of His atoning sacrifice, and, in virtue of the eternal covenant subsisting between Him and the Father, thereby obtains for those who come to Him by faith the application to their souls of the saving efficacy of His atonement. Moreover, when, from time to time, they fall into occasional sin, He is their Advocate with the Father, and, in virtue of His atonement once for all offered for all sin, procures for them remission of the special transgressions into which, through the frailty of their nature, they have fallen. "If any man sin"—if any believer in Christ fall into particular acts of sin—"we have an Advocate (a Paraclete or Intercessor) with the Father, Jesus Christ the righteous." As the Son of Man, the sharer of our nature, with all its sinless infirmities, and, moreover, tried and tempted in all things like as we are, our Divine Mediator is specially qualified to discharge this function of intercession. His experience of human infirmity, human suffering, and human temptation, enables Him to have a fellow-feeling, a bond of sympathy, with the weak, the suffering, and the tempted. Objections, no doubt, have been urged, and difficulties there unquestionably are, as to how a Being, perfectly holy and free from all tendencies to evil, can, in any proper sense of the word, be said to have been tempted like as we are. These difficulties and objections I cannot now stop to consider. It would lead us into discussions foreign to our present subject, and demanding long and careful attention. Suffice it to say that the difficulties have been removed and the objections answered, quite sufficiently for all practical purposes, and quite as far as we could even hope for, taking into account the profoundly mysterious nature of the subject, the union in one person of perfect God with perfect Man.

Neither shall I stop to enquire why an experimental acquaintance with the infirmities and trials of our nature should be necessary (as St. Paul so plainly asserts it to be, in the passage which I have already quoted from the second chapter of this Epistle to the Hebrews,) in order to move the sympathy of Him who, as our Creator, knows what is in man, all the weaknesses of his nature, and all the difficulties of his position; of Him, whose boundless love and compassion it was which, in the first instance, prompted Him to assume our nature: why it "behoved Him to be made like unto His brethren in all things," in order that He might be a "merciful High-Priest:" and why an actual familiarity with suffering and temptation should be requisite in order that He should be "able to succour them that are tempted." These are questions which cannot now be discussed. I shall only observe, in general, that there may possibly be something in the very nature of a Being completely happy, and wholly removed from the sphere of temptation and suffering, incompatible with the perfect exercise of that kind of sympathy and compassion which is involved in the notion of an Intercessor or Advocate, such as our blessed Lord is described to be. The presence of a *human* element may, for anything we can tell, be essential to the perfect discharge of that office. It is remarkable that our Lord's office of Universal Judge is also connected—and that, too, by Himself in very explicit terms—with His *human* nature: "The Father judgeth no man, but hath committed all judgment to the Son..... The Father hath given Him authority to execute judgment, because He is the Son of Man." The reason, or at least part of it, is well expressed by Bishop Pearson: because of "His affinity with their nature;" because of "His sense of their infirmities;" because that "His appearance in this human form is most fit to represent the greatest mildness and sweetness of equity in the severity of that just and irrespective judgment."

Again, as "every good gift and every perfect gift is from above, and cometh down from the Father of lights," so it is through the mediation and intercession of the Lord Jesus that such gifts are bestowed upon men. This office of the triumphant Messiah was foreshadowed in that prophecy of the sixty-eighth Psalm, which St. Paul quotes in the fourth chapter of his Epistle to the Ephesians: "When He ascended up on high, He led captivity captive and gave gifts unto men." The Psalmist, under the inspiration of the Holy Spirit, represents Jehovah Himself, the God of Hosts, after having subdued His enemies, as ascending in triumph the heights of Zion, and receiving as a conqueror the gifts of the vanquished and tributary nations. These gifts or spoils He then distributes, as eastern conquerors were accustomed to do, among His own people. But those words of the inspired Psalmist had a further and a deeper meaning, which the inspired Apostle was enabled to unfold. They foreshadowed the future victory to be achieved by the Son of God, when, having conquered sin and death and hell, He should ascend to the highest heavens, and, as the fruits and trophies of His victory, shed forth spiritual gifts, whereby His Kingdom should be established in the world, and His faithful people throughout all time be cheered and strengthened and sustained. As the Victor, upon His Throne, He is the Mediator through whom are dispensed all the spiritual gifts and blessings which are shed forth on each and every member of His Church. He is "the Head, from whom all the body by joints and bands having nourishment ministered, and knit together, increaseth with the increase of God." The gift of the Holy Spirit, to abide for ever with His Church, was the first and most precious fruit of the intercession of Christ, after His ascension to the throne of the Majesty in the heavens; "I will pray the Father, and He shall give you another Comforter, that He may abide with you for ever." The intimate relation and interdependence which subsist between the mediatorial office of Christ in heaven and the operations of the Holy Spirit in the Church on earth, explains why it is that St. Paul, in a well-known passage of the Epistle to the Romans, calls the Holy Spirit "the Spirit of Christ;" and it further explains why our blessed Lord is so often described as the Dispenser of those spiritual gifts which, in the economy of salvation, it is the direct and special function of the Holy Ghost to impart. And well may our glorified Redeemer be regarded in this light, seeing that the infinite merits of His atonement are the ultimate source and efficient cause of all the spiritual blessings which the world enjoys; seeing that vital union with Him is necessary in order that the outflowings of Divine grace, through the ministration of the Holy Spirit, may reach each individual soul; and seeing, lastly, that He is the supreme Ruler of His Church, God having given "Him to be Head over all things to the Church, which is His Body, the fulness of Him that filleth all in all."

Again, Christ, on His Throne, as the Mediator between God and man, hears our prayers and answers them. We offer up our prayers at the throne of grace *to* Him, as "very God of very God;" *through* Him, as the channel whereby we have access unto the Father; and *in* Him, as the spiritual sphere, the holy element, in which every petition is to be offered, and every knee is to bow. Every temporal and spiritual evil that we deprecate, every temporal and spiritual good that we desire, is averted or conferred (so far as it seemeth good to His godly wisdom) by Him, and through Him, and in Him. Brethren, what a blessed thought it is, that, amid all the sin and suffering and sorrow which we see around us in the world; amid the trials, disappointments, and afflictions with which it may be our own lot to have been visited; what a blessed thought it is, that there is One "who is able to save to the uttermost those that come unto God by Him, seeing that He ever liveth to make intercession for them!" What a comforting thought that our great Intercessor can be touched with the feeling of our infirmities! The same principle which prompts us, when exposed to suffering and trial, to rely most firmly on those who have themselves suffered and been tried, leads us to confide implicitly in Him who shared all our sorrows, and who "in all our affliction was afflicted." Our reason, indeed, may be convinced that a good and merciful Creator will not try us unnecessarily, and beyond our powers of endurance; but our feeling of sympathy irresistibly impels us to believe that One who was tried and tempted in all points like as we are, will not inflict upon us a single superfluous pang, and will, moreover, "with every temptation also make a way to escape, that we may be able to bear it." When, in the hour of suffering and trial, we look for human consolation, we do not seek it at the hands of the careless, the gay, the happy, or the stoical. We desire to pour our griefs into the ear of that friend who, we know, has had his own trials and afflictions, and who can, therefore, enter into our thoughts and understand our feelings. And so, when we look for higher consolation than earthly friends can offer, what an inestimable blessing and privilege it is that we have, enthroned above, a Mediator, a Friend, a Brother, who was Himself pre-eminently "a man of sorrows, and acquainted with grief," and "was tempted in all points like as we are, sin alone excepted."

That merciful and sympathizing Mediator "is able to save to the uttermost"—completely and for ever—"those who draw near to God through Him," by that "new and living way which He hath consecrated for us, through the veil, that is to say, His flesh," seeing He ever liveth to make intercession for us. That mediatorial intercession with His Father shall continue until the complete redemption of God's people shall be accomplished, when sin shall be utterly abolished, Satan finally vanquished, "death swallowed up in victory," "all tears wiped away," suffering and sorrow brought for ever to a close.

Such, brethren, is the mediation of the Victor, on His Throne. Its foundation is the sacrifice and oblation offered once for all by the crucified and ascended Jesus: its motive, the infinite love and compassion of Him who has borne our griefs, and shared our sufferings and trials; its effect, the continued preservation of His believing people during their journey to their heavenly home, and the removal of every cloud which sin from time to time interposes between them and their Father's countenance. The perpetual mediation of Christ in heaven bears the same kind of relation to the work of redemption which He accomplished on earth, that God's perpetual providence bears to the original creation of the world by Him.

Seeing then, brethren, that we have a great High-Priest, who has passed through the heavens, and taken His seat on the right hand of the throne of God, there to remain as the Mediator, Intercessor, and Advocate of His people, until He shall come again in His glorious Majesty to judge both the quick and dead, let us hold fast the confession of our faith and of our hope without wavering; and let us come boldly to the throne of grace, that we may obtain mercy, and find grace to help in time of need.

To those who come humbly trusting in the merits of their crucified Redeemer, this mercy and grace will be vouchsafed in *every* time of need. Most comfortable words these, but they also convey a very solemn warning, which must not be lost sight of. I cannot convey it better than in the words of St. Chrysostom: "The Apostle has well said '*seasonable* help' (εὔκαιρον βοή-θειαν); that is to say, If you come now to the throne of grace, you will obtain mercy and find grace; for, in that case, you come seasonably or opportunely. But if you defer coming to some future time, the result may be otherwise. Your approach then may be too late; for then it may be no longer the throne of grace. It is the throne of grace so long as the King sits dispensing grace; but when the day of grace is over, He ariseth to judgment." Here, then, we have, along with the comforting assurance arising from our knowledge of the tender sympathy of our merciful Redeemer and Intercessor, a solemn warning also not to abuse His long-suffering and compassion. There is "an *acceptable* time;" there is an "*opportune* help." But that time is the *present*; that aid is offered *now:* "I have heard thee in a time accepted, and in the day of salvation have I succoured thee: behold, now is the accepted time; behold, now is the day of salvation." An inspired Apostle has described that terrific scene which shall take place when they who have not sought mercy at the throne of grace, shall, in the agony of their despair, exclaim to the mountains and rocks, "Fall on us, and hide us from the face of Him that sitteth on the throne, and from the wrath of the Lamb."

May the Spirit of God dispose each one of us, my fellow-sinners, to "seek the Lord while He may be found, and to call upon Him while He is near!" May He enable us to "flee for refuge," at once, and "to lay hold upon the hope set before us!" That hope we shall find, amid all the trials and sufferings of this chequered scene, to be a "sure and stedfast anchor to our souls," uniting them to Him who, on our behalf, has entered within the veil, and there, the Victor over death and Satan, sits enthroned, our great High-Priest, our sympathizing and never-failing Mediator, Intercessor, and Friend.

SERMON VII.

The Victor, on His Throne, the Priest of His People.

HEBREWS vii. 26.

"Such an High Priest became us, who is holy, harmless, undefiled, separate from sinners, and made higher than the heavens."

THERE is nothing which has to do with religion so world-wide as the institution of Priesthood, and necessarily so, if religion be a social thing—if under its influence men come together to worship God with any sort of common worship. If the original idea of religion had been disintegrating—if from the first it had taught men that the most acceptable worship of God is that each one, alone, by himself, should worship God without temples, altars, courts, then there would have been no room for priesthood of any sort; but if religion in its idea be a uniting thing—if men under its influence have from the first come *together* to worship God, then they must have some one to act for them towards God.

If a multitude meet together to offer a common sacrifice, there must be some one to kill the sacrifice, or to sprinkle the blood, or to apply the fire, or to do that, whatsoever it be, upon which they agree to think that the acceptance on God's part depends.

Again, if they come together to offer up united supplications, or to acknowledge mercies received by all, there must be some one to lead, if the common utterance is to be anything beyond a confused murmur.

But there is another universal principle connected with religion, considered as intercourse with God, which also has upheld in all forms of worship of all nations the priestly idea, and that is the sense of sin.

The universal conscience of mankind bears witness to some natural alienation between God and man; that God and man are not at one, that there must be some intercessor for men, who is not, in all respects, one of themselves.

But who is he that is to act such a part? Who can speak for his brethren from a standing not their own?

Evidently it must be one who whilst one of themselves is still in some sense separate from them.

Hence the universality of consecration. If he who is to act for his brethren cannot be naturally separate, since God has made all men of one blood, men will separate him in some way; they labour to give him a factitious separation; they set him apart by the holiest rites that can be devised; they clothe him with a special robe; they ordain that he shall be of one tribe or cast, or else that he shall not marry; they forbid him to eat with his brethren,—anything, provided that it will separate or distinguish him.

So that, whilst his participation in the common nature enables him to be the ambassador of his brethren to represent them with God, there may yet be that about him which may help men to realize (or to imagine) that in some sense he comes from God and acts for God.

Such is the principle of Priesthood, having its roots deep struck into the ground of all common intercourse between God and man, and that intercourse, so far as we are concerned, the intercourse of sinners with God their Judge.

So that the idea of Priesthood seems to be inseparable from the religious consciousness of the human race.

For all the religions or superstitions which lay claim to remote antiquity, or seem to embody any part of the early religious traditions of the race—Pelasgic, Etruscan, Egyptian, Persian, Hindoo, Gothic, Celtic, even the Mexican and Peruvian, as well as those of the Islands of the Pacific—recognise Priesthood. There is none in which the idea of Priesthood in some shape is not imbedded.

It is impossible to get rid of it.

It lingers when the idea of God is almost extinguished. It re-appears in those adaptations, or reformations, or perversions of old faiths which have taken firmest hold of nations and races, such as Buddhism and Mahometanism. It cannot be eliminated from Christianity without denying the Christian ministry altogether. The one sect, the Friends, who have most thoroughly and consistently repudiated all Priesthood, have got rid of all ministry and all Sacraments as well.

They who retain wholly, or in part, the idea of the Christian ministry, and yet would fain reject the idea of Priesthood as connected with that ministry, cannot do so. Their own discipline and worship witness against them. Not only do they, as a rule, rigorously confine the ministration of the Sacraments to those who have had some sort of ordination among them, but in one point they even go further than the Catholic Church in the direction of Priesthood; for, as a rule, the minister who conducts the worship of Presbyterian or other similar bodies conducts it by himself. It is supposed to be his sole composition at the time, and is undoubtedly uttered by him alone. The people having no frequent share in it, nor making it their own by response.

So that they who would fain get rid of Priesthood as connected with the ministry, end in depriving the people, as priests of God, of their due share in what ought to be the Church's common utterances.

Priesthood, then, is inseparable from the religion of sinners, i.e. from the religion of our race; at least from any form of it which has not utterly severed itself from the past, or professes to inherit any traditions whatsoever—Primitive, Jewish, or Christian.

And now, how came this idea amongst men? We know not, just as we know not (so, that is, as to speak with certainty) how the idea of Sacrifice became so universally prevalent. But it must have come in one of two ways:—Either God gave special directions to the first family, so that they heard the voice of the Lord God telling them that when they came together they must approach Him by sacrifice, and that the highest or holiest amongst them must perform this service for his brethren, and that as they increased and multiplied, they must set apart a family, or tribe, or order, so that the service of God should not be the occasion of strife and debate; or God acted in this matter more impalpably: He simply convinced men's conscience of sin, so that they desired to draw near to God in solemn worship, not alone, not one by one, but in the company of their fellows,—so that each individual sinner might be less noticeable; and if so, there must be one chosen out from among them to speak for them in prayer, and to sprinkle the blood of the sacrifice.

But no matter how the priestly idea arose and gained ground, it must have been from God, or God could not have stamped it with sanctions so marked as He has done.

If Priesthood among men were from beneath, not from above, God would not have directed His first great servant, whom He called His Friend, to bow before Melchizedec for his blessing; nor would He have separated one tribe from among His people to "be His priests, to come near to Him, to offer upon His altar, to burn incense;" nor, above all, would He have permitted His servants to ascribe priestly functions to His Only-Begotten.

No, my brethren, it cannot be that the religious consciousness of mankind—first embodied in all Gentile tradition, and then sanctioned and purified by Jewish or Christian revelation—should be wrong.

If the conscience of mankind in this matter of Priesthood has been wrong, then there is no religious conscience at all; no such thing in the world as religious instinct.

But if this principle of Priesthood be, as we have every reason to think that it is, a gleam from the true light which lighteth every man that cometh into the world, then, in all confidence, we may take it to be a part of the "education of the world;" not the secular education of the world for the reception of a human philosophy, however excellent, but the religious education of the world for the saving reception of the truth of the Person and office of Jesus Christ.

It fulfils in this respect the same work as the universal prevalence of Sacrifice, the same work as the universal belief in supernatural interferences.

There was one principle underlying every ancient

faith, which was that the gods can interfere, and have interfered, with the visible order of things, for the purpose of manifesting themselves in kindness or in wrath; and unless there had been an universal diffusion of this idea, so as to make it conceivable at least by all, how could men have ever been called upon to entertain the idea of the Incarnation? If the sequence of nature had never been broken, or if the dim distorted memory of Divine interferences had been allowed to perish utterly, how could men have received such books as the Gospels? The miracles of Jesus would have been powerless either to convince, or even to teach. They would have had nothing to appeal to. They would have been like the forms of letters to men who could not entertain the idea of an alphabet.

And so with Sacrifice.

In some mysterious way the Death on Calvary cleansed the very world. "What God hath cleansed," said the voice from heaven to one who as yet realized not the acceptance of the Gentiles in Christ, "What God hath cleansed, that call not thou common."

Unless the New Testament be from end to end an utterly misleading book, the crucified Body of the Redeemer was to be, from the moment of the consummation of the sacrifice, the source of all cleansing, all reconciliation, all forgiveness.

But how could the human mind be in a condition to receive such ideas? Simply, we answer, through its education by sacrifice. By far the clearest setting forth of this great truth, that the sacrificial system was the greatest element in the religious education of the world for the reception of the atoning power of the death of Christ, comes from the pen of one who (strange to say) denies the expiatory nature of that death. "In the facts (of the death of Christ)," he says, "outwardly regarded, there is no sacrifice, or atonement, or oblation, or propitiation, but simply a living and dying thus and thus..... How shall we come to God by help of this martyrdom? How shall we turn it, or turn ourselves under it, so as to be justified and set in peace with God? Plainly there is a want here, and this want is met by giving a thought form to the facts which is not in the facts themselves. They are put directly into the moulds of the altar, and we are called on to accept the crucified God-Man as our sacrifice, an offering or oblation for us, our propitiation; so to be sprinkled from our evil conscience, washed, purged, purified, cleansed from our sin. Instead of leaving the matter of the facts just as they occurred, there is a reverting to familiar forms of thought, made familiar partly for this purpose; and we are told to use the facts just as we would the sin-offerings of the altar..... According to the Epistle to the Hebrews, the ancient ritual was devised by God, apart from its Liturgical uses, to be the vehicle in words of the heavenly things in Christ, moulds of thought for the world's grand altar-service in Christ the universal Offering....

"And so much is there in this, that without these forms of the altar, we should be utterly at a loss in making any use of the Christian facts that would set us in a condition of practical reconciliation with God. Christ is good, beautiful, wonderful, His disinterested love is a picture in itself, His forgiving patience melts into my feeling, His Passion rends open my heart; but what is He for, and how shall He be made unto me the salvation I want? One word—He is my Sacrifice—opens all to me, and beholding Him, with all my sin upon Him, I count Him my offering, I come unto God by Him, and enter into the holiest by His Blood[a]."

And so with Priesthood.

The Priesthood of Christ is that aspect of His whole mediatorial work with which, as sinners, we have first and most to do.

Christ is our Mediator. He is our great mediating Prophet, Priest, and King. And God has so ordered the constitution of this world's society, that in each of these functions men might comprehend, and so receive His acting.

Men, for instance, may be all naturally equal, but if from the first there had been nothing but a dead level in human society, all office proceeding from and held at the mere will of the people, how could men have been able to receive such a kingship as that of the Redeemer? It was for this; that men might in due time own the everlasting rule of Christ, that "The pageant of earthly royalty has the semblance and the benediction of the Eternal King."

And so with Christ's Priesthood. Christ's mediatorial work has not only to do with our instruction as our Prophet, and with the ordering of all things for us and in us as our King, but it has above all things to do with the putting away of sin, the cleansing of the worshipper, so that the remembrance of past sins may not keep him from God, and hinder or mar his service.

The universal religious instinct of mankind, as well as direct revelation, have taught that repentance is not sufficient of itself. There must be purification from some *thing* out of ourselves, and there must be some *one* to dispense or apply the purification with the authority of that God whose law has been outraged.

[a] Dr. Bushnell on Vicarious Sacrifice, p. 460.

And as the sacrificial idea, with its accompanying vocabulary, prepared men for the sacrifice of Christ; so the idea of priesthood, inextricably intertwined with it, prepared the world for the reception of the fact that the Son of God, having procured for us forgiveness by the sacrifice of Himself, would Himself be, in His own Person, on His throne, the minister of His Father in dispensing that forgiveness.

Christ is the Priest of His people.

All other priesthood is but a shadow of His. The God-ordained Jewish priesthood was the shadow which, though without life, still preserved the outline.

The various priesthoods of heathendom are like the dim disjointed shadows in turbid and troubled water, but still in them His Priesthood is discernible, in both men have a something which enables them the more readily to accept Him as their Priest.

I trust that the time has not been lost in this attempt to shew the hand of God in the diffusion of this world-wide religious form. There are those in our midst who would deprive the Church of the reality of the Redeemer's Priesthood, i.e. they would deprive the sinner of that office of Christ which has especially to do with the forgiveness of his sins, and the communication of God's grace to him.

They would throw us back upon natural religion. They would discredit all in Christianity in which there is "progress" beyond natural religion. Well, then, in this matter of Priesthood, Christianity is but the answer to the inarticulate prayer of universal human nature.

The religious aspirations of the race are not what men develope in their studies, but what corresponds with the facts of universal history and human life.

And the prayer of human nature in all its tribes has been but the "Amen" to that of Israel of old: "Speak thou with us, and we will hear; but let not God speak with us, lest we die."

The function inherent in true priesthood is twofold: the priest pronounces blessing from God on his brethren, and he offers up to God the prayers, the praises, the sacrifices, or Eucharists, of his brethren.

So it was with the first priest on record. "And Melchizedec, King of Salem, brought forth bread and wine: and he was the priest of the Most High God. And he blessed him, and said, Blessed be Abram of the Most High God, possessor of heaven and earth: and blessed be the Most High God, which hath delivered thine enemies into thine hand. And he gave him tithes of all." Here Melchizedec, on the part of God and as His ambassador, blesses even the father of the faithful, and offers up to God blessing on the part of the father of the faithful, for his victory, and receives in God's stead his thank-offering of the tithe of all. And so with the Jewish high-priest. He blessed the people in the name of God, and he received at the people's hands the sacrifices which they offered up to God. It was because he, or those under him, offered them to God on His altar, that there was any atonement attending the offering; but of this reconciliation or atonement he was of course only the minister or dispenser. It all came from God.

In the fulness of time appeared the great Highpriest. The One only Priest who has the truth of the office inherent in Himself. The One Priest whose blessing from God is all-availing, and whose intercession with God is all-prevailing.

He, our one perfect Priest, if He is to fulfil the idea

of perfect priesthood, must be at once one with sinners, and yet separate from them.

One with sinners, so that He may be on their side, and act for them towards God; and yet separate from sinners, so that we may regard Him as truly coming from God, and identified with the cause of the All-Holy, so that He may with the authority of God act from God towards us.

All this meets in Him.

He is one with sinners, for He has taken part in their flesh and blood. He has a human soul as they have, having the passions of such a soul, having all its sinless infirmities. In the days of His flesh He hungred, He thirsted, He submitted to the will of His own creatures; He suffered grief, so as to weep over Jerusalem; He wept for very sympathy when He saw others weep, as at the grave of Lazarus. He was one with sinners, too, in the consequence of their sin, in pain, in agony, in desertion of soul, in death.

And with all this He was separate: so far as regards the union of the two natures there was, of course, within Him the abyss between the uncreated and the created, the infinite and the finite. He could act for God, on God's part, on God's side because He is God, and so is identified with all that is in God; as, for instance, with God's severity as well as with His mercy, for who has ever revealed the extreme wrath of God against sinners as Christ has revealed it. And as regards His human nature—that in which He is one with us—He is also separate; marvellous, blessed mystery, one and yet separate. One with us, in that He is "perfect Man of a reasonable soul and human flesh;" a reasonable soul that in the days of its probation tasted grief, disappointed hopes, desertion, every bitter thing that a pure soul can taste : and yet separate, for whereas every other soul of man has been vanquished by sin and evil, He was victorious.

In this one point is His separation for His priestly work. For though in His Father's councils He was separate from eternity, though He was separated in the womb and from the womb by the Spirit of God, though He was solemnly consecrated at His baptism, yet all this would have been utterly unavailing if He had been for but one moment one with His brethren in their subjugation by sin. He would then have needed a priest, or intercessor, or mediator, for Himself.

But He was the Victor in every conflict. We are ever to remember that though at one particular crisis He was brought face to face with the Evil One, and was compelled to hold converse with the arch liar and murderer, when the devil was permitted, as it were, to treat with Him for the dominion of the world ; yet that we are by no means to limit His victory to the issue of this conflict, or even to the issue of the final conflict in His victory over death.

His whole life was one conflict.

Did it cost Him no struggle, He who was from the first dawn of consciousness filled with wisdom, to live thirty years the life of an obscure artizan in a country town of a half-civilized province; so veiling His astonishing powers that they who were of His own flesh and blood, certainly those who had been in familiar intercourse with Him from His childhood, were astonished beyond measure when they first heard Him expound the Scriptures ? Was there no struggle, whilst such latent powers were pent up within Him, to wait for so many years His Father's time for His full manifestation? No struggle to Him to live these many years in unknown and unnoticed obscurity, attracting little, perhaps no more attention than any other good but poor man in a similar state of life?

Yes, we may be sure that there was a conflict and a victory here; and that this victory did its part to separate and sanctify Him to be a Priest capable of sympathizing with the myriads of His brethren, who have to dwell in poverty and obscurity, unknown and unregarded, under subjection, depending for their subsistence upon the will of employers.

So that in this, and doubtless in many other matters, His private life was a conflict and victory.

Again; when He began a more public life, was there no struggle and victory in His every-day intercourse with the Twelve? Surely there is a hard conflict to maintain persevering patience revealed in such words as —" Why reason ye because ye have no bread, perceive ye not yet neither understand, have ye your heart yet hardened, having eyes see ye not, and having ears hear ye not, and do ye not remember; how is it that ye do not understand?"

And is nothing of conflict revealed in that almost bitter exclamation: "Oh, faithless and perverse generation, how long shall I be with you, how long shall I suffer you?"

And this conflict and victory must have been a daily one; increasing, apparently, not diminishing, until His final victory over death. Nay, even after His resurrection we find a trace of it: "Oh fools," He says, "and slow of heart, to believe all that the prophets have spoken."

In ways like these we may see clearly how the whole life of the Son of Man was a struggle and victory:

a struggle, having its more glorious scenes of triumph in the wilderness, and in the judgment-hall, and on the cross ; but, after all, a conflict which had His whole life for its battle-field.

And thus was He, in the nature which He had assumed, "separate from sinners." Thus did it become Him, for whom are all things, and by whom are all things, in bringing many sons unto glory, to make the High-priest of their salvation "perfect through suffering."

It became Him to give us such a Priest, and such an High-priest became us; for our Priest was not to be a mere outward Priest, whose work was the manipulation of external rites and outward forms of cleansing. No; He was to be the Reconciler and Restorer of souls. He was to apply His forgiveness, His consolations, and His sustaining grace, to each one of His brethren according to his need. His priestly work has a twofold aspect, whether we regard Him as acting towards God or towards His brethren. Towards God He has to act by presenting towards His Father His Church and its united prayers, supplications, Eucharists, and praises: He is her mouth to speak for her, and in her name, towards God. And He has also to intercede with His Father for each soul, ("Lord, let it alone this year also"). He has also to present to His Father, and to perfume with His merits, the intercourse of each soul with God.

In this consists the twofold aspect of His Priesthood, in that the transactions of each soul in His Church with Him is twofold. Each soul comes to Him individually, by itself, and unburdens its griefs, its sufferings, its falls and sins to Him, as if there were no one in the Universe except Him and her; and yet, if His word is to be trusted for one single truth, each soul must come to Him in and through the ministrations of His Church, as one of an innumerable multitude, knit together in a mystical body under Him as its head, all joined together in one organization as branches of Himself, the living Vine.

And in each of these cases the Church, or the soul, comes to Him as the true and only Israel, the Victor Who, after a life-long struggle and wrestling, prevailed; won from God the blessing of all blessings, the eternal life of those in Him.

And as He acts on the behalf of His Church and of every individual member of it towards God, so, corresponding to this, is His acting on behalf of God towards His Church. It, too, is twofold.

Through His ministers, the dispensers of His word and Sacraments; and towards each soul individually. Through His under-priests He is at once the universal Baptizer, the Confirmer, the Confessor, the Absolver, the Dispenser of His Body and His Blood.

When we come to Him through His ministers for grace in these rites of His Church, it may be well for us to remember that the grace which He dispenses He won. It was given to Him as the reward of His victory in a life-long conflict.

And He won it for us.

Oh, it may make us more careful to prepare our souls to receive His grace, if we remember that He had to purchase the power of giving it to us from God by an infinite humiliation; and this humiliation not a momentary act, not once for all accomplished, but in which He had to maintain a strife through long years of hard usage, sorrow, disappointment, contempt, and scorn.

K

And it might subdue our souls to esteem more highly His gifts of grace, and to examine more carefully how we grow in them and profit by them, if we realized more that He, the Victor Priest, gives them to us in order to ensure to us, if we hold fast His grace, the victory over the same enemies.

He, the Victor, dispenses to us His grace in order that we may be partakers with Him in the victory.

He conquered death for us, and so it is a faithful saying: "If we be dead with Him"—if we be partakers with Him in His death to sin—"we shall also live with Him."

He attained to this victory by a life of suffering, and so the faithful saying ends not there, but continues—"If we suffer, we shall also reign with Him."

Oh, then, when we approach the Sacrament of His Body and Blood, let us have before us not only the heavenly and spiritual presence of the Bread which comes down from heaven, but His own personal presence as the Dispenser.

Behind the earthly ministering priest is the heavenly One; and He, as the Victor, strengthening our souls for the same conflict which He endured against the same foes by that Flesh in which is life, and in which He conquered. We see the hand of His ministering servant, but it is but the instrument of another hand which reaches to us the bread of life,—the hand of the Omnipresent Victor.

And when in the same Eucharist we shew forth His death till He come again, let us realize that when we "do this" in these His courts below, we are joining in that one eternal Eucharist of His own blessed presence, of His own blessed Body, marked with the wounds which He received when He gained the victory over the last enemy, which is ever being celebrated at the right hand of God in heaven.

And so also with the secret approaches of the soul to Him. When we come to Him in self-denial and fasting, we come to One Who nerved His human nature to conquer by these weapons, and can teach us how to use them, and impart to us of His power, so that in Him we should be conquerors. When we, looking to Him, treasure up His *word* in our hearts, so that with it we may drive back the enemy, as we humbly use this sword of the Spirit we gain more confidence from the thought that, in the use of it, He too was more than Conqueror, and that for us.

When we plead in prayer His promised intercession, it may make us more careful, and more persevering, if we remember that He won a blessing for us by more than prayer, by "strong crying and tears to Him that was able to save Him." And when we meekly accept reproach and suffering for His sake, and strive to regard it as a partaking of His Cross, it may give us more patience and endurance, and, perhaps, more joy under it, to remember that by the things which He suffered, He won the knowledge of *the* obedience—$\dot{\eta}$ $\dot{v}\pi\alpha\kappa o\dot{\eta}$—that special obedience by which He became perfected as our sympathizing and consoling High Priest.

And, lastly, are we His Priests? Bear we His commission to preach, to teach, to baptize, to feed, to lead, to defend His flock; or is this ministry the object of our hopes, and of our prayers? How can we be His efficient priests, if we be not ourselves, in our poor way, victors?

If we are conquered by the love of pleasure, of ease, of refined society, of amusement, or by vain glory, or by the desire of preferment, or by party spirit, or by the world in any of its manifold shapes, or by the flesh in any of its manifold cravings, how can we be the instruments of the Victor Priest for the conveyance of His conquering grace to His brethren in their conflict?

We may, it is true, convey His grace *officially*. God in mercy to His flock will see to it, that the pledges of His grace are to true hearts what He designs them to be to all, even at our hands; but in all that is not strictly official, in all that needs heart and soul, how can we represent our great Victor Priest to His struggling fellow-members!

Oh wonderful, oh most wonderful insight into the deepest relations of the Victor Priest, through His under priests to His people, in the Evening Hymn of Him whom God since last Lent has removed from His militant Church.

In that hymn we have a precious litany of supplication, for the ark of Christ's Church, the civil rulers, the priests, the falling, or unconverted; the sick, the poor, the mourners: and what is the one supplication for the priests of Christ?

> "Oh, by Thine own sad burden, borne
> So meekly up the hill of scorn,
> Teach Thou Thy priests their daily cross
> To bear as Thine, nor count it loss."

SERMON VIII.

The Victor, on His Throne, giving Gifts to Men.

EPHESIANS iv. 7—12.

"But to every one of us is given grace according to the measure of the gift of Christ. Wherefore he saith:—When He ascended up on high, He led captivity captive, and gave gifts unto men.
"Now that He ascended, what is it but that He also descended first into the lower parts of the earth? He that descended is the same also that ascended up far above all heavens, that He might fill all things. And He gave some, apostles; and some, prophets; and some, evangelists; and some, pastors and teachers: for the perfecting of the saints, for the work of the ministry, for the edifying of the Body of Christ."

THE Christians of Ephesus lived within sight of the temple of Diana, "whom all Asia and the world worshipped[a]." Inside the temple was a black image of the goddess, which was reputed to have fallen from heaven[b]. Hither flocked crowds of pilgrims, who, on returning home, were accustomed to take with them miniature models of the shrine in silver[c] or other metal. Thus Ephesus became the centre of a vast system of heathenism;—one of the chief instruments employed by the "rulers of the darkness of this world" to hold men down in spiritual bondage.

From this system believers in Christ had separated themselves. By doing so, they appeared to the heathen

---

[a] Acts xix. 27. [b] ver. 35. [c] ver. 24.

world to have given up everything that adorned humanity, or made life itself desirable. They became, to pagan eyes, so many detached atoms; without any principle of cohesion; out of communion with earth and heaven.

In reality, how different from all this was their state! These seeming outcasts had, in fact, been incorporated into a society, which is destined to embrace both heaven and earth in its unity.

The Son of God had descended to this lower world, and taken on Him our nature, that we might "have redemption through His blood[d]." Then He "ascended up far above all heavens, that He might fill all things[e];" sending forth His new-creating Spirit to raise the spiritually dead, and to gather them into living unity with Himself;—thus forming, as out of the dust of the earth, that "Church, which is His body[f]."

To this Church, or congregation of faithful men, Christ, the ascended Saviour, stood in the closest relationship. As every particle of the body is in vital connexion with the head, and contributes to the well-being of the body, so every Christian, even the very humblest, had "grace given to him, according to the measure of Christ's bounty," and contributed something to the well-being of the Church.

The analogy extended yet further. As the bodily life is upheld by means of certain organs and channels of circulation,—such as nerves and arteries,—so is it with the Church. When Christ "ascended up on high," He provided certain *special gifts*, which He left behind for the Church's nourishment and conservation. What were these GIFTS?

---

[d] Eph. i. 7.   [e] Eph. iv. 10.   [f] Eph. i. 22, 23.

Were they (as some have dreamt[g]) moral or intellectual endowments,—justice, courage, wisdom, philosophy, or the like? No: says the Apostle,—He took *from among men* those whom He "*gave to men*" as the special channel of His blessing. "He gave some (to be) apostles; some, prophets; some, evangelists; some, pastors and teachers." These were His own chosen *gifts*.

So, says St. Paul, was realized, in its full dimensions, that which had been set forth in historical type under the elder Covenant; that to which the great Pentecostal Psalm referred[h], where it says, that when the Lord "ascended up on high, He led captivity captive, and gave gifts unto men."

To see the meaning of this more clearly, we must go back to the commencement of Israel's existence as a Church.

When God "came down[i]" with visible glory on Mount Sinai, amidst myriads of angels[k], He formally established the Abrahamic covenant[l], and adopted Israel to be His people. They were to be to Him "a kingdom of priests[m];" and He would "*dwell among them*[n], and be their God." For this end He instituted "the Tabernacle of Congregation," (or "of Meeting"); for "*there*," said God, "I will meet with the children of Israel; and it shall be sanctified by My glory." The spiritual life of the nation was bound up with this holy Tabernacle.

But observe how the life was to circulate from it. It was by means of one tribe,—the Levites,—whom God

---

[g] See, e.g., the painted altar-piece of Christ Church, Marylebone.
[h] Psalm lxviii., which was sung by the Jews at the Feast of Pentecost.
[i] Exod. xix. 18, 20, xxxiv. 5, (LXX. $κατέβη$; cp. Eph. iv. 9).
[k] Deut. xxxiii. 2; cp. Ps. lxviii. 17.   [l] Gen. xvii. 7.
[m] Exod. xix. 6.   [n] Exod. xxix. 42—45; cp. Ps. lxviii. 16, 18.

"*took* out of the midst of the sons of Israel," to be "*given* to the Lord to serve the service of the Tabernacle of Congregation º." He first *took* them, as His own, "wholly given to Himself;" and then He *gave* them to Aaron and the Church "for the work of the ministry" in the Tabernacle ᴾ. As soon as Canaan was occupied, the dedicated tribe was distributed throughout the country, both east and west of Jordan; so that by its means the Tabernacle of God virtually spread itself over the whole land. By the Levites, then, "as by joints and bands, the whole body" of Israel, "having nourishment ministered and being knit together," was to "increase with the increase of God ᑫ."

Let us now return to the Pentecostal Psalm, quoted by St. Paul.

This majestic ode was written to celebrate God's goodness in dwelling among His people Israel. He, whose name was "YAH,"—the 'Self-Existent,'—condescended to care for that poor nomad horde in the wilderness. He even took up His abode among them, in the centre of their encampment. This was their strength in conflict;—"God arose, and His enemies were scattered ʳ." This gave them possession of Canaan. This kept them in it through the period of the Judges ˢ. This enabled David to triumph over Israel's enemies. And now God had been pleased to allow His Ark to be carried up to Mount Sion. There, on lowly Sion, His presence was granted as really, though not with the same accompaniments of visible glory, as it

---

º Numb. xviii. 6. (LXX. ἐγὼ εἴληφα ... τοὺς Λευίτας ... δόμα δεδομένον Κυρίῳ).

ᴾ Cp. Numb. iii. 9, viii. 9—19. (At ver. 19, the LXX. have, καὶ ἀπέδωκα τοὺς Λευίτας.)

ᑫ Col. ii. 19.   ʳ Ps. lxviii. 1; cp. Numb. x. 35.

ˢ Ps. lxviii. 12—14.

once was at Sinai. He did not now choose the ministrants of His sanctuary—"the Tabernacle He pitched among men [t]"—from the ranks of the "twice ten thousand angels" who formed His retinue at Sinai [u]:—He took them "*from among men.*" From among men He took them,—rebellious men,—that even here on earth, "the Lord God might have a home [x]."

This was wondrous condescension: scarcely credible, indeed, were it not that that "Tabernacle of Meeting" prefigured a yet deeper mystery,—that meeting of God and man, which was effected when "the Word was made flesh and dwelt (tabernacled) among us [y]." In Christ "dwelt all the fulness of the Godhead bodily [z]." He descended into the conflict with sin, and death, and hell; and after "triumphing over them openly [z]," He took from amongst His redeemed some, whom He made over as His own gifts to mankind, "for the perfecting of the saints, for the work of the ministry, for the building up of the Body of Christ." "He gave some, apostles; and some, prophets; and some, evangelists; and some, pastors and teachers."

The statement in my text, then, clearly implies what St. Paul's view was of the Church,—the "tabernacle, which the Lord pitched, and not man."

(1.) High beyond all thought, and invested with unapproachable dignity, stands our kingly Priest;—exalted "far above all heavens," yet in intimate union with us on earth;—presenting before the mercy-seat His most perfect sacrifice and intercessions on behalf of all His penitent, obedient, self-consecrating people.

And here below are (2.) His Levites;—not *priests;*—forbidden, indeed, "to come near the vessels of the

---

[t] Ps. lxxviii. 60. cp. Numb. xviii. 15.) [u] Ps. lxviii. 17. [x] ver. 18. (On *ba*-adam,
[y] St. John i. 14. [z] Col. ii. 9, 15.

sanctuary and the altar[a];"—but given to Christ, and by Christ, for the salvation of men; "ministers of Jesus Christ, ministering the Gospel of God, that the offering up of the nations may be acceptable being sanctified by the Holy Ghost[b]." In brief, the work of their ministry is "to make ready a people prepared for the Lord[c];"—that these may be "built up a spiritual house, a holy priesthood, to offer up spiritual sacrifices, acceptable to God by Jesus Christ[d]."

Thus, brethren, "the Tabernacle of God is with men, and He dwells among them[e]:"—not, indeed, manifested in terrible majesty, as on Sinai; but ruling with effective power, as from Sion;—ruling so that even the world's outward history gives at least indications of His presence.

Is not this the reason why that portion of mankind which is called Christendom is by far the most advanced, the noblest, the most replete with living energy? We confess that in all Christian nations there are many who adhere only to the outside of the Church;—but the elevated character of the collective mass is unquestionable; and this is primarily due to the working of the Church inside it.

And whence came this Church? We all know. It dates its birth from the day of Pentecost which followed our Lord's ascension. It sprang forth suddenly;—a new Creation. Its own averment (and there is no other credible account) has always been, that Jesus, "being

---

[a] Numb. xviii. 3.
[b] Rom. xv. 16. λειτουργὸν Ἰησοῦ Χριστοῦ, ἱερουργοῦντα τὸ εὐαγγέλιον. On which Bengel rightly notes, "Jesus est sacerdos; Paulus sacerdotis minister."
[c] St. Luke i. 17; cp. Coll. for 3rd Sunday in Advent.
[d] 1 St. Pet. ii. 5; cp. ver. 9, and Exod. xix. 5, 6.
[e] Rev xxi. 3.

exalted by the right hand of the Father, and having received from the Father the promise of the Holy Ghost, poured forth" the stream of miraculous influence, which on that day amazed Jerusalem.

From that epoch the various ministers of the Church began to work. *Apostles* stood forth as Christ's envoys, commissioned to "Christianize all nations;" to lay the foundations of the Church; to establish by their acts and their writings the model on which all after generations were to mould themselves. *Prophets* gave utterance to high religious truth, whether in the form of expositions of Scripture or in hymns and prayers. *Evangelists* were enabled to communicate the Gospel to strangers; as *pastors* and *teachers* were to feed and instruct settled congregations.

By these agents (Christ working through them) the Churches of the first age were formed and consolidated; —many Churches, and yet One;—all being bound together in their common relation to "Him which is the Head, even Christ."

But how, when we leave that first age? Did Christ's "gifts" die out, or did He raise up a continuous succession of them?

In general, it is most evident that there has all along been a body of men known as "the Lord's portion," *clerus Domini*, the Clergy. These have claimed to be, and have been regarded as, Christ's ministers. They have traced up their authority and spiritual lineage to the Apostles. With their health or sickness the Church has prospered or languished. If doctrinal error or practical corruption got entrance among them, the whole body suffered decay; when they were sound, then by them, "as by nerves and arteries," religious life circulated through the system.

Although, then, (like the Levites of old,) they may often have deviated from the rule laid down for them must we not still regard them as Christ's "gifts?" And, as a matter of fact, do we not find that, in a very considerable degree, their history presents us with a continuation of the apostles, prophets, evangelists, pastors, and teachers of the First Age?

(1.) The office of *Apostles* could not, from its very nature, be in its fulness transmissible. For they were to speak of Christ as eye-witnesses; to testify what Christ had entrusted to them personally; to lay the foundations of the Universal Church; to be the pillars in God's temple, on which the "great mystery of godliness" should stand recorded to all ages. This was necessarily peculiar to themselves.

Yet they ordained men to take up and perpetuate their work. They appointed bishops, who were to bear rule in the Apostolic federation, and to feed the Church of God with Apostolic doctrine, as embodied in Scripture.

We know how carefully the Episcopate did for many centuries watch over this sacred deposit. The spirit that animated them was that of Irenæus, who wrote, "The Apostles handed down to us in the Scriptures what was to be the pillar and ground of our faith [f]." To these Scriptures they adhered as their sole rule of faith. "We are resolved," said Athanasius, "to hear nothing and to say nothing beyond that which is written [g]." This was the resolve which swayed the great councils of bishops that assembled in defence of the faith in the best times.

Through long and weary ages this order of bishops has survived: and still amongst ourselves its work is

[f] Adv. Hær. iii. 1.   [g] De Inc. Christi [i. p. 484]

to maintain the succession of Apostolic doctrine and discipline. When a bishop is consecrated, a Bible is delivered to him with the words, "Think upon the things contained in this book." When a bishop ordains presbyters or deacons, he puts a Bible or a New Testament into their hands. Thus from generation to generation the Apostolic word is committed to living witnesses;—as in Israel, the Law of Moses, placed by the side of the ark, was entrusted to the keeping of the Levites[h].

In a recurrence to this Apostolic deposit, brethren, is all our hope of attaining to any wholesome peace or Church-reformation at the present day. When Christians shall turn from their weak dependence on the traditions of human schools, ancient or modern, and receive the teachings of Christ's own Apostles in their plain and undiluted meaning, then will the Holy Spirit —(does not "the residue of the Spirit" still abide among us?)—work His full work without let or hindrance. Then believers, being joined "in the Apostles' doctrine and fellowship," shall again be "of one heart and one soul."

(2.) The work of *Prophets* was to build up the Church by unfolding the interior sense of Scripture, or by other devotional utterances.

And in what age have there not been men (chiefly among the clergy) whose insight into the meaning of God's Word, and whose skill in evolving that meaning,—in homilies, prayers, hymns, or other forms,— have been such as to make us thank God for them?

Has not the Church had in them a continuation of the prophetic grace?

(3.) The function of *Evangelists* was to carry the

[h] Deut. xxxi. 25.

glad tidings of God's love to people who had not heard of it. At first this was, of course, done without written Gospels; but when Scripture had taken form, chiefly by its help.

So Eusebius[i] describes the work of an Evangelist as being to "preach Christ and deliver the Scripture of the Holy Gospels." And speaking of Pantænus, (who went as a missionary to India,) he calls him, "an Evangelist of the Word[j]."

To procure acceptance for the written Word was at all times an important part of the missionary's work. It is recorded that when our own Wilfred visited Rome, before he went out as missionary to Thuringia, he collected numerous copies of the Scriptures there, and brought them away "at the cost of no slight toil[k]."

And now that the Church has begun again to "stir up" the evangelistic grace within her, we have the same temper exhibited. The work of translating the Gospels, of transfusing their meaning into the vernaculars of pagan races, is now going on in every part of the world. It is a work for which men of very special endowments are required. Let us pray God to bestow them upon us in larger abundance.

(4) Of the work of *pastors* and *teachers* I need not speak. Beyond all controversy this office has existed, and still exists. Each person, to whom it is committed, solemnly professes beforehand his belief that he is inwardly moved by the Holy Ghost to take it upon him;—in other words, that he is Christ's own "gift" to the Church.

Thus, then, my brethren, down to the present time, men have been raised up to guard the Apostolic deposit, to quicken the Church's understanding of Divine

---

[i] H. E., iii. 37.   [j] v. 10.   [k] Non modico labore.

mysteries, to carry the Gospel to the heathen, to watch over and instruct the faithful. And these "gifts" of the ascended Saviour have (in spite of man's shortcomings) availed to the "edification of the body of Christ." Through them "the Lord God has had His dwelling" on earth. Millions of souls have by their means been united into one holy temple. Baptized into the blessed Triune Name, they have owned *one Lord*, been sanctified by *one Spirit*, and adored *one God and Father of all, who is above all, and through all, and in us all.*

God's covenant has not been broken. His "word has not returned to Him void."

Too often, indeed, Christ's Levites have not retained their fidelity; so that to them the old reproof[1] might be addressed: "Ye have corrupted the covenant of Levi." Too often have God's Nazarites, instead of being "purer than snow," had "their visage darkened [m]" with famine of the word of God, and the oppression of the great enemy.

God's grace no more precludes the working of man's free-will now than it did under the Old Covenant. Within forty days of the giving of the Law on Sinai, the Israelites, with Aaron at their head, had fallen back into Apis-worship. Within forty years after the consecration of the temple, Solomon was seen bowing down to Milcom and Ashtoreth.

Yet God's "gift" to Israel was not in vain.

So it is now. Jesus, our Mediatorial King, is seated in heaven dispensing gifts unto men,—"gifts" that are taken from among men. Though these *may* "corrupt themselves[n]," yet His purposes shall never be frustrated. "The gates of hell,"—its council chamber and its legions,

---

[1] Mal. ii. 8.   [m] Lam. iv. 7, 8.   [n] Deut. xxxii. 5.

—"cannot prevail against" Christ's Church. "God is in the midst of her; she shall not be moved." Age after age souls are still being prepared for a more glorious "inhabitation of God;" when all the sanctified shall be gathered into the perfected Church, which shall be "the fulness of Him who filleth all in all."

My brethren, the meditation we have been engaged in has been a very solemn one. I trust it may not have been unprofitable. It will not be so, if it lead us to think with deeper reality of Christ's manifold working in His Church.

His "gifts" are still with us. Let our faith gratefully acknowledge their presence, and diligently profit by them. Let them serve to bind us in union to Him from whom all our spiritual life comes. He is the "Apostle and High-Priest of our profession;" He—the Prophet of His Church, "in whom are hid all the treasures of wisdom and knowledge;" He—the Light "to lighten the heathen;" He—the Chief Shepherd and Bishop of souls. He is "the Head, from whom the whole body, fitly joined together, and compacted by that which every joint supplieth, according to the effectual working in the measure of every part, maketh increase of the body to the edifying of itself in love."

To Him, with the Father and the Holy Ghost, ever one adorable God, be ascribed all honour and glory through all ages. Amen.

SERMON IX.

The Victor, on His Throne, mystically United to His People.

ST. JOHN xvii. 10.

"And all Mine are Thine, and Thine are Mine, and I am glorified in them."

THE subjects of this series of sermons have hitherto had in view our Lord in His own Person alone, though Himself as the centre of infinite energies of life. They regard Him in His own pure individuality as acting on or for others in the manifold spheres of the spiritual life. The subject which has been committed to me involves the contemplation of Him in His intimate connection with His elect; His individuality merged in the oneness of His mystical Body,—what Holy Scripture describes under a term scarcely possible for us to comprehend in its full meaning, "the Fulness of Him that filleth all in all[a]." It is Himself no longer as one, but losing Himself in another unity, the perfected communion of His elect people.

Our Lord in His Incarnation acts as the medium between the invisible God and the creatures. It was necessary, according to the design of eternal Love towards the creation, and for the perfecting of the bliss and holiness of the creatures, to constitute a link to bind,

[a] Eph. i. 23.

to unite them with God. Our Lord supplies this link in His own Person. The complete purpose of the Incarnation is fulfilled in the final ingathering and reunion —to use the Scriptural term, the "reconciliation"—of all the elect creatures, and our Lord is the principle of reunion, the Reconciler of all orders of intelligent beings throughout the entire range of created life, which circulates to and fro around Him, as it emanates from Him, and pervades and unites all the separate individuals who are to be taken up into this entireness of a blessed Unity in the consummation of bliss through the accomplishment of the predestination of God.

Our Lord in the text expresses the fact of His being thus the One medium of union between the Father and the elect. This is the primary meaning of the words, "And all Mine are Thine, and Thine are Mine." He is, through the operation of the Eternal Spirit, both the cause and bond of this union. The extent to which it reaches forth on every side, is revealed by St. Paul, as e.g. in the Colossians, where Christ is represented to be the cause of the first creation, as it was projected forth from God, creating life to be dependent on God through Him. He describes our Lord as the Image, the visible manifested form or expression of the invisible God: "For by Him were all things created, that are in heaven, and that are in earth, visible and invisible, whether they be thrones, or dominions, or principalities, or powers: all things were created by Him, and for Him: and He is before all things, and by Him all things consist [b]."

Afterwards the Apostle reveals the subsequent truth that Christ is likewise the Restorer of the Creation after the Fall, the cause of the reunion of what had been separated from God by sin: "For it pleased the Father that

[b] Col. i. 16, 17.

in Him should all fulness dwell ; and, having made peace through the Blood of His Cross, by Him to reconcile all things unto Himself; by Him, I say, whether they be things in earth, or things in heaven[c]." The whole vast circumference of created being revives in the union of love which, centring in Christ, diffuses itself so as to take up and absorb into itself all true angelic as well as all true human life.

But human life has its special distinctive glory in the midst of that all-glorious mystical Body of which Christ is the Head and Heart: "He took not on Him the nature of angels ; but He took on Him the seed of Abraham[d]." There is a oneness between Christ and His own elect among men, through their common nature, which is peculiar to man. Where do we read anything with regard to angels in their relation to our Lord, like to what St. Paul speaks of as the end of the ministry on earth of Apostles, Prophets, Evangelists, pastors, and teachers? It was ordained, as he declares, "for the perfecting of the saints, for the work of the ministry, for the edifying of the Body of Christ: till we all come in the unity of the faith, and of the knowledge of the Son of God, unto a perfect man, unto the measure of the stature of the fulness of Christ[e]." St. Paul describes the result to be that the whole body of the redeemed from among men form but one man, that there is but one individual, as it were, compacted together, composed of the multitudinous individual souls of men, our Lord having His part with us in the complete Humanity—for he speaks of Him as the Head, and the rest, His own elect people, as the members of this one complete Body. And this idea runs throughout Holy Scripture ; for separate individual men are compared to the eye and the hand, and the

[c] Col. i. 19, 20. [d] Heb. ii. 16. [e] Eph. iv. 12, 13.

foot, each one being not a whole, but part of a whole, members in a body, all together making the one man, the compound man in Christ, in which Body nevertheless every one, as Christ Himself, preserves his own separate individuality.

Man's nature commenced in oneness of life. Eve dwelt in Adam's side before she came forth into separate existence. The Creator, while Adam slept, took one of his ribs, and formed the woman. It was a parting away of part of himself, that from the separated existence of the one humanity existing in the pair, there might grow as out of one the multitudinous races, still one in their origin, in their separate individualities diverging infinitely. And, again, this original division was designed only that these separated individuals might again return into oneness in the new Adam. This returning is effected as each individual life—after living apart for a while, and feeling its own loneliness, and longing the more to be one—finds its rest again in the perfect Man. Each individual experiences itself to be but an imperfect being, not able to live alone, because not good for it to be alone, and discovering this truth in the conscious helplessness of his lonely struggles with the burden of his life, hastens back to the opened side, His side which bled for him, and, as it bled, opened the new way, through the "rent veil which is His flesh," to return to God in Him Who is both God and Man in one, for man's own sake, that all might be one again in Him. Man's troubled life is thus a cycle proceeding from unity in the first Adam, and then through endless division returning into unity again in the second Adam. The first unity is in the earthly embryo, an undeveloped state existing only in the possibility of a perfect life, as Christ Himself was once "in the loins of Abraham when Melchisedech met him." The last unity will be a conscious existence of perfection in Him, as though His Godhead were become one's own individual personality, with all the thrilling fulness of perfect powers in oneself, corresponding with the love and joy, the peace and holiness, developed in the glorified life of Jesus in His Victor form of power on His throne, at His Father's side, as we in Him, and Himself in all, are glorified together.

Further, this closest union of all life in Christ, so peculiar to man, has an importance in God's design far beyond our own special glory and bliss in Christ; for our union in Him forms the basis, the underlying inner principle on which all other creatures are reconciled and united with God. The human nature has a ground of union with God, of which no other nature is capable. The angelic natures in their varied orders are represented in the Revelations circling around the inner Unity of the One Incarnate God, as all lower natures still further off from the throne of God circle around them; but the saints formed on earth are "in the midst of," as well as "around the throne" of the Victor. Angels are only "around the throne," and there are creatures yet beyond, while man alone is "in the midst of" its mysterious majesty of ineffable glory[1].

And this truth was the real cause of the importance of all that passed on earth while our Lord, yet visibly present in the flesh, was drawing to Himself the first disciples whom the Father gave unto Him. For it was not merely God's own drawing. The will of those who were drawn must necessarily coincide with His own will, according to the laws of responsible creatures. They

[1] Rev. iv. 6.

must believe and see, and yield their own natures, as truly as God draws them. And there was, therefore, an indescribable anxiety hanging on the results of those first drawings through which, in the days of His flesh, our Lord was attracting souls to Him, and in Him to the Father. During the first two years of His ministry there was no sign of any such real union. His followers crowded around, and pursued Him even for days in the wilderness; but yet any single hard saying was enough to cause whole multitudes to fall back. The one idea which pervaded even the Apostles' minds, was the Jewish view of the earthly kingdom, the reign of the Victor on Mount Zion, in the national exaltation manifesting some earthly millennial glory. Of the mystical body, of the inner life of the spirit-world in intimate union with God, in the home of light and perfect love, there was no gleam of anticipation, no thought. Nor indeed could there be, for there was no basis on which it could rest, while as yet the hidden Godhead of the Son of Man was unrevealed. This shews how much hung on the question which at last—but not until two full years of the ministry were expired, and the time was rapidly drawing towards the end—our Lord put to the Apostles, "Whom do men say that I, the Son of Man, am?" The answer even then gave no hope that the very first foundation of the mystical union was as yet laid among the people. "Some say, Thou art John the Baptist, some Elias, and others one of the Prophets[r]." All was as yet dark. No foundation as yet was gained in the heart of man for the future unity of God and man; for faith in the Godhead of Christ was the very first condition of the restored unity. Then was uttered the critical question as to the Apostles themselves, which, if

[r] St. Matt. xvi. 13, 14.

this had failed also, would still have left all in doubt. But the desired answer came, and its eventfulness, if we bear in mind what hung upon it, it is impossible to exaggerate: "Peter answered and said, Thou art the Christ, the Son of the living God [h]."

We can understand the rising up of the heart of Jesus, rejoicing at this reply, because here was the first indication of the truth having entered into the hearts of those who were to form the nucleus of the future communion of saints, the first-fruits of the working of the life which He had come to form in union with Himself when He should return in His ascended Majesty to His throne. Therefore the great blessing fell on him whose lips had uttered it: "Blessed art thou, Simon Bar-jona; for flesh and blood hath not revealed it unto thee, but My Father which is in heaven." Nor did the words of blessing cease, but it continued on, the strain of triumphant anticipation still breaking forth from the lips of Jesus, as He marked this commencement of living faith, and saw developing in the future the complete mystical Body of the elect around His throne: "And I say unto thee, Thou art Peter, and upon this rock I will build My Church; and the gates of hell shall not prevail against it [i]."

Consider, again, this same truth as the interpretation of that intensity of feeling which our Lord evidently experienced when the Greeks came to Him, desirous of seeing Him. As soon as their coming was announced to Jesus, there arose from His lips expressions of joy and victory, unaccountable except from this same cause: "And Jesus answered them, saying, The hour is come, that the Son of Man should be glorified [k]." He saw in these representatives of the heathen world the ingather-

[h] St. Matt. xvi. 16.   [i] Ibid., 17, 18.   [k] St. John xii. 23.

ing of the faithful of the whole Gentile races into His mystical Body, which was in truth His own glorification. He saw, He felt the inner bond of union being knit, already drawing these few, because they were to Him the first realization of the consciousness of the countless followers of all times and nations, who in the opening future, by a mutual embrace in the deep yearnings of spiritual love, would at last be united to Him; to be the witnesses and sharers of His triumph on His throne, in the great Day when He would perfect the hosts of His redeemed from among men. The scene brought vividly before the mind of our Lord the whole results of His atoning Death, and the final reconciliation to God of all creatures. "Verily, verily, I say unto you, Except a corn of wheat fall into the ground and die, it abideth alone; but if it die, it bringeth forth much fruit[1]."

It is by considering this same eventful issue then at stake that we may discern the cause of the earnest, anxious care with which in the same night in which He was betrayed by one Apostle, our Lord guarded the others who abode faithful, from the possibility of falling away under the approaching trial to which their hearts would be exposed, during the last crisis of His Passion. For what if these should fall away? What if these few, who formed the only nucleus of the future Church, were to forsake Him, and return no more? Consider how He used that night persuasion, encouragement, promises, to fortify, to prepare them! See what warnings He gave, what clear, earnest revelations of the future, that they might be forearmed against the peril before it came to pass, that "when it was come to pass, they might believe." And may we not see arising within the heart

[1] St. John xii. 24.

of our Lord a feeling of relief, even a triumphant expectation as He felt how His power would work in Peter's soul, as the representative of the rest of the Apostles, in saving Him from the uttermost fall: "I have prayed for thee, that thy faith fail not; and when thou art converted, strengthen thy brethren [m]."

Surely this was one main cause why our Lord so "greatly desired to eat this Passover" with them before He suffered; a desire that they should be fitted to receive aright that mystical Presence of Himself; a desire to impart Himself to them as the Sustenance of their frail humanity. For now they would be strengthened; now He had actually accomplished the first stage of that mystical union which He had come to form between Himself and them. That Passover was on this account to our Lord a special rest, because it was the pledge and assurance of a sustaining power that they could receive, and which, if truly received, would uphold them under the terrible crisis of the approaching Crucifixion. One received to his greater condemnation; but the rest "to the strengthening and refreshing of their souls," and thus though falling partially, they yet remained secure in the "strength of that meat" in which they would be enabled to ascend to the truer Horeb, the real "mount of God."

That first Eucharist was the token, the foreshadowing of what would in fuller measure continue in ceaseless operation throughout the world, when on His throne, His victory accomplished, the Victor would shed forth everywhere His glorified Humanity, through His Spirit. The great intercessory prayer, of which the text is the central idea, is throughout one prolonged pleading for the completeness of the union then com-

[m] St. Luke xxii. 32.

menced, to extend and develop through all time into eternity, as its true home of bliss. "I have manifested Thy Name unto the men whom Thou gavest Me. Thine they were, and Thou gavest them Me.... I pray for them, for they are Thine. And all Mine are Thine, and Thine are Mine, and I am glorified in them.... Neither pray I for these alone, but for them also which shall believe on Me through their word. That they all may be one, as Thou, Father, art in Me, and I in Thee, that they also may be one in us, ... and the glory which Thou gavest Me, I have given them.... I in them, and Thou in Me, that they may be made perfect in One.... Father, I will that they also whom Thou hast given Me, be with Me where I am, that they may behold My glory which Thou hast given Me, ... that the love wherewith Thou hast loved Me may be in them, and I in them"[n].

These last words lead us to consider how this life of mystical union with our Blessed Lord is partaken of and perfected, now that He has ascended to His throne of glory.

Bear first in mind that it is here on earth, in our present state, this union commences, wherever the true conditions are fulfilled. Let us consider some of these conditions, and first such as are independent of the sacramental means through which they are wrought.

First, there needs a living faith in our Lord's true Divinity equally as in His true Humanity. This primary faith is essential to our union with Him. For the ground of union is His Godhead, by which alone He can reconcile to Himself all creatures. It is not merely a figurative, a metaphorical idea of which we speak, when we speak of the mystical union of Christ and His elect. It

[n] St. John xvii.

is not a union as of men bound by common ties and mutual interests, not even a union as of man and wife, which though indissoluble except by death, is yet but a oneness of mutual dependence and common duties, and consecrated rights binding the one to the other. This closest tie of earth, though sacramental, is but a type and symbol of a yet more august and more sacred union.

The union of Christ with His elect, is a union of mutual indwelling, a working together of one life, and one heart beating in its infinite pulsations through the One body, and while yet retaining its separate individualities of existence, is itself an individuality as really as if there were but one soul in one body. And how could this be but by the operation of Divine power, by that which is infinite, supernatural, superlocal, pervading, interpenetrating the finite, the natural? And how can we participate of this but by faith? "The just shall live by faith." It is only to be accomplished by the coalescing of souls animated and transformed by grace, with the indwelling Presence of the Son of God manifest in the flesh; as St. John says, "That which was from the beginning, which we have heard, which we have seen with our eyes, which we have looked upon, and our hands have handled, of the Word of life; that which we have seen and heard declare we unto you, that ye also may have fellowship with us; and truly our fellowship is with the Father, and with His Son Jesus Christ°." Without the full reception of the Godhead through the soul's true faith in Him, this mystical union has no groundwork, no living subsistence. He must be recognised as the Victor, eternally co-equal with the Father; otherwise no substratum is laid for the possi-

° 1 St. John i. 1, 3.

bility of such a union; there is no true meeting-point between God and man. In no other true sense could He say, "All Mine are Thine, and Thine are Mine." Nor can we be among the "Thine," except through the faith by which the Father draws us to Himself by the Son.

Secondly, there must in this fellowship be the union of heart and will, of thought and desire. It would be a mere mechanical union unless the mutual intelligence meet and intermingle. Our Lord and the Father are One, because of the perfect union and correspondence existing between them, in their will equally as in their substance. Could there by any possibility have been any divergence of the will of Jesus from the will of the Father, the unity would have been dissolved. "All Mine are Thine." This was through all His course the one great principle of life. "I come to do Thy Will, I am content to do it, yea, Thy law is within My heart [p]." "The Son can do nothing of Himself, but what He seeth the Father do [q]." There was the complete inner union, the unvarying oneness of mind. And the same must extend itself also to His members, His own elect. It must be equally true that, "All Thine are Mine;" all who are drawn by Thee to Me, are made one with Me in mind. The mystical union is unreal and practically fails, if this moral union exists not. Can we claim oneness, any real portion in the mystical Body of Christ, if the temper, the desires, the joys, the will, the affections are permanently and essentially at variance with Him; if there be no tendency in the uncertain, wavering lines of life to converge; if there be no effort to meet? There is, indeed, a real mysterious intercommunion of grace between the

[p] Heb. x. 7.   [q] St. John v. 19.

several individual members of the mystical Body of Christ, one being linked to another in common bonds of life, and having a common share in the One Life. Our Andrewes teaches that in the "Communion of Saints there is the mutual participation in sanctification vouchsafed to every member of that mystical body." But this unity in grace implies oneness of mind, and we fall off from the mystical body in proportion as we become spiritually out of harmony with the true members of the body, and so out of harmony with Him as Head of the body. How can we be truly and vitally in Him unless we are among those whom He owns, among the "Thine" who are "Mine,"—if it could be said of us, "your thoughts are not My thoughts, neither are your ways My ways, saith the Lord [r]?" If there be conscious sin unconfessed, not put away; if there be any allowance of a known evil habit; if evil thoughts prevail unresisted, unsubdued, becoming habitual; if the character have taken a wrong bent or tone; if the constant tendency is against, not for, Him and His cause, not seeking to copy His example in His union with the Father; if we are diverse in habits of mind and heart, when compared with Him, how can it be but that the union involved in our regeneration, must practically grow less and less, till it becomes a very mockery, and a ground of hopeless condemnation?

Thirdly, as this moral union is required to form an inner living reality, so this again requires a continual increase of life, through actual participation of our Lord. This is the ground on which rests the need of the constant reception of the Holy Eucharist. This blessed ordinance is at once the great means of bestowing the mystical life, and the anticipative realization of the per-

[r] Isa. lv. 8.

fected union hereafter. He who is the very central Life of the whole mystical Body imparts Himself to all in His divine Communion, uniting all with Himself, and through Himself with each other. It is a pause in our earthly course when the longed-for union knows no let, no hindrance. It is a time when even here on earth Heaven and earth are one; when the Victor from the Throne and the earthly captives of His grace, meet; when all variances and discords of mind and heart are for the moment silent; when all the movements of each separate member of the body are at rest in one heart-thrilling consciousness; when the power of the Highest possesses, enfolds, enwraps, enchants each and all with a common glory; when there is but one thought, one consciousness, one vision, one pervading power, one pure joy, thrilling with a uniform pulse throughout the whole body; when the mystical union is complete and undisturbed,—the Eucharistic Presence through the overshadowing of the Holy Ghost, being over us, around us, within us, reconciling all in one, absorbing together Himself the very Head, and ourselves, His members, now filled with Himself, and living in His fulness. It is then that this unity is for the time, as an anticipation, fulfilled; —when it may be truly said, "All Mine are Thine, and Thine are Mine." Our Lord and His faithful are then indeed for the time glorified in one. "We are one Body, for we are all partakers of that one Bread*." It is heaven begun in a very truth, only how soon to lose that completeness, as again we fall; and yet the same perfect life to be again and again realized, even though not possible to be kept perfect and undisturbed in the complete possession of an indefectible grace, though with power to grow ever more and more, as we increasingly feed on

* 1 Cor. x. 17.

Him, and abide in Him. We are, as we communicate, really lost to the consciousness of time and space; all mere sense of the creatures and of nature is passed away for the moment, and it is as though already God were All in all; as though the unity which pervades the Blessed in Heaven, had suddenly spread itself forth to flood the earth, as an advancing tide overflows its bounds by a sudden rush, and though to retreat again, yet again and again to return. Such is the blessedness and the need of constant and fervent reception of the Blessed Sacrament. Our life becomes thus a life of grace in nature, overpowering nature. It is Christ formed in us, and through Him, the whole blessed Trinity. "If a man love Me, he will keep My words: and My Father will love him, and we will come unto him, and make our abode with him [t]." It is the forming within us of the glory which exists first in the Humanity of Jesus, which broke forth in His Transfiguration as for a moment, and is now in its full and stedfast radiance clothing Him on the throne, and by His Spirit spreading and communicating itself through all the elect, as they become by grace capable of receiving Him.

Such, then, is our present dignity, in proportion as it is realized in us, making us one with God, linking us with all true created life in God; hidden within us, but yet even now our only real life, by which we already rise, and live above space and time in the Infinite and the Eternal.

What would life become more and more, if we lived more and more in the power of this consciousness? What our present share in the glory which, encircling His Throne, is overshadowing and indwelling secretly

[t] St. John xiv. 23.

on earth all true hearts? To attain this should ever be our fervent, earnest, longing, as we "press forward to the things that are before," "if by any means we may apprehend that for which we are apprehended of Christ Jesus." What need of watchful care, of unceasing, stedfast studying of the life and spirit of Jesus? What a call ever sounding in our hearts to put forth increasing efforts for the attainment of His mind! What utter loss if we fail! What unspeakable, endless blessedness, if at last we are found faithful, and in Him, the Head and centre of this life, are accepted!

SERMON X.

The Victor, on His Throne, absolving His People.

ST. MATTHEW vii. 29.

"For He taught them as one having authority, and not as the scribes."

ST. JOHN xx. 23.

"Whose soever sins ye remit, they are remitted unto them; and whose soever sins ye retain, they are retained."

WE cannot wonder that the Jews were unable to see the greatness of the Majesty which in Christ was concealed under a human form, and that they could not at once distinguish between Him and the crowds of scribes and philosophers who came, each with his theory, to find acceptance with the people.

Men would not at once recognise the claims of one, who had received no instruction, to speak with an authority greater than that which the scribes presumed to claim. Yet this claim to authority gives our Lord's words their distinctive character: He does not proclaim that, which men may accept, or reject at their pleasure; but absolute truth, which those who reject, reject at their peril: and He asks from all an obedience so entire, that those who knew His mother and His brethren might well say, "Whence hath this Man these things; and who gave Him this authority?"

And if His claims seemed to be extraordinary, it must be admitted that the prophecies which formed the Jewish conception of a Messiah were somewhat confusing; there was in the coming Christ a double character; in the fifty-third chapter of Isaiah it says, "When we shall see Him there is no beauty that we should admire Him." In the sixty-third another note is struck, and at sight of Him the prophet says, "Who is this that cometh from Edom, with dyed garments from Bozrah? this that is glorious in His apparel, travelling in the greatness of His strength." There is a coming one, but He is now, a sheep led to the slaughter, and now, the Conqueror treading the wine-press in His wrath.

This double character exhibited in the prophecies is very observable in our Lord's life; and there are occasions in that life when the sufferer and the conqueror are presented together in a very striking manner. Our Lord's endurance is probably too exclusively dwelt upon by us: and we thereby get a mistaken notion of the manner of man He was. There were endurance and suffering; but there was aggression too: He was the Lamb led to the slaughter; but He was, too, a Conqueror; He bore the taunts and insults of Pharisees and Sadducees; but He dealt back shafts of rebuke and withering satire, which, destroying the people's faith in their old leaders, shattered the crystal fabric of Pharisaism in which the fossil forms of a once living faith were imbedded. He never appeared to the leaders of the Jews to be a patient sufferer until He hung as their victim on the cross. He was rather a daring aggressor, rooting up all things that had received the sanction of ages. The Pharisees had lived in the respect of the people, and the teachers had been called Rabbi; and when He denounced against them the woes of the twenty-third chapter of St. Matthew, He must have seemed to them not a meek sufferer, but a formidable enemy that must be crushed. And they judged Him rightly; for they had felt His power; they had experienced His withering satire, and saw Him enter the streets of Jerusalem accompanied by the shouts of those who once had recognised *their* leadership and called *them* Rabbi, but now cried to Him "Hosanna; Blessed is He that cometh in the Name of the Lord: Hosanna in the Highest." It was not by endurance only that He took their place in the affections of the people.

On several occasions while we seem to be looking at the Man of sorrows we start back at hearing the voice of the Victor. His disciples felt themselves to be in the presence of the Man of sorrows, when they, wishing to help Him, said, "Lord, shall we smite with the sword?" They felt themselves in the presence of a Conqueror, voluntarily suffering, when He said, "Thinkest thou not that I can pray to My Father, and He shall presently send Me twelve legions of angels?"

Pilate seemed to be speaking to His victim when he said, "Knowest Thou not that I have power to condemn Thee, and have power to release Thee?" but it was the Conqueror's voice which said to him, "Thou sayest that I am a King. To this end was I born, and for this cause came I into the world."

He was the enduring sufferer in Gethsemane and on the cross; but it was to a King the thief addressed the petition, "Lord, remember me when Thou comest into Thy kingdom;" and it was the Conqueror's voice which answered, "This day shalt thou be with Me in Paradise."

The life of Christ is the life of the Man of sorrows; but it is, too, the life of the hero cleaving his way to victory: the difference between Him and worldly heroes being, that one fights with the chances of victory or death, the other gains victory in death; that death, who discrowns kings and strips the laurel from the victor's brow, placed upon His brow the unfading laurel of victory. Pilate wrote on the cross in mockery, "This is Jesus the King of the Jews;" Death turned the sarcasm into a prophecy. The Man of sorrows cried, "My God, my God, why hast Thou forsaken Me?" the Victor, Conqueror in death, bowed His head, and said, "It is finished."

After His resurrection, one of these elements is gone —the double character ceases. He is then the Victor giving laws to the kingdom He has purchased; speaking to His disciples of the kingdom of heaven, and giving them the commission in the language of authority, "Go ye into all the world, and preach the Gospel to every creature. He that believeth and is baptized shall be saved; but he that believeth not shall be damned."

He spoke to the Apostles the things concerning His kingdom; and He bids them tell men to observe all the things He had commanded. He proved from Scripture that repentance and remission of sins must be preached to all nations, and He shewed how they were to be remitted when He said, "Whosoever sins ye remit, they are remitted unto them; and whosoever sins ye retain, they are retained." And He shewed that this authority was intrusted to the whole body of the Church, when He told them to refer all disputed questions to the Church, and promised Himself to ratify the decision of that Church[a]. It is the voice of the Victor forming and organizing a kingdom; giving with authority laws to guide that kingdom, and giving the Church authority over its members by the promise that their decision should be His decision. It is sufficiently clear

* St. Matthew i. 17, 18.

that Christ formed a kingdom, and that this authority to absolve or remit sins was committed to the body of that kingdom, to be exercised under proper restrictions by the executive of that kingdom. What that kingdom is, I proceed shortly to consider.

I shall but be stating a simple historical fact when I say that, since our Lord's time, a kingdom professing to have sprung from Him has existed in the world, and that the progress and growth of this kingdom is the most important fact of the last 1800 years. It has retained all the marks by which the continuity of a society may be proved: it has had in all countries a definite and distinct method of admission to its offices, and a fixed form of government; it has held a definite and distinct creed, and owned Christ as its universal King. And this kingdom is not a mere invisible society, or an abstract idea, but a very tangible and visible organization: for as an abstract thing, unembodied in a system, Christianity never has had an existence, while the system itself has been, and is, the most important element in human society. The persecutions of early ages were not directed against mere abstract principles, but were intended to decimate and destroy a very visible and very tangible kingdom. The savage chiefs of the Middle Ages, in their contests with the Church, knew they were not contending with a mere phase of opinion, but, as they found to their cost, with a very visible and very tangible power; and the concordats of the present day are attempts to adjust the relationship between the secular officials of kingdoms and the officials of an organization whose living presence is felt and recognised. The difficulties between what are called Church and State arise from the existence of the officials of a kingdom who recognise laws as binding upon them which do not form part of the laws or systems of any mere political systems.

And this very visible kingdom is the outgrowth of that society which Christ established; if Baptism was then the one only mode of admission, it is the one only mode now; if in early times each new branch organized itself as soon as practicable under the episcopal form of government, as the mode which Christ had provided, episcopacy is the universally accepted form of government now; if the laying on of the hands of the presbytery was then the one mode of admission to its principal offices, it is the one mode adopted now. There is no break in the continuity of the kingdom; it has been, and is, a corporation having branches all over the world; propagating one creed, with one universal form of government, and one only mode of admission to its offices. And if our Lord said, "Whose soever sins ye remit, they are remitted unto them; and whose soever sins ye retain, they are retained," it is quite certain that ever since that time and now, it has been, and is, the faith of the Catholic Church that this power and authority is the heir-loom of the kingdom until He shall come again.

I do not deny that at times the Church has used its power unjustly, and sometimes unwisely, and that in it there has often been a strange mingling of truth and superstition: this is only what our Lord led us to expect, but it was a kingdom Christ came to found, and a kingdom the Apostles went forth to found, and the growth of this kingdom is, I repeat, the great fact of the last 1800 years. Truth during that period has been more or less mingled with error, the error however, as years have gone by, existing in a constantly decreasing proportion. The Scriptures have been more or less, but with an ever-increasing power, studied and accepted; Christianity has been more or less mingled with error and superstition; the kingdom has been with varied intensity in different countries, but on the whole with a deepening intensity penetrated with its own principles, but the kingdom itself is a living fact. And this is exactly what the New Testament leads us to expect; the point kept before us is not the universal acceptance of the Scriptures; we are nowhere told of the immediate elimination of error, or of lower forms of truth; the kingdom is the burden of our Lord's discourses, the object of His parables, the work of the Apostles, and the great fact of 2000 years, and now in its widely-extended bounds 260 million people find a home, while Christian sects who have separated from it do involuntarily yield to it the homage of respect and superiority.

Where, if this Holy Catholic Church is not the Kingdom of Heaven, is that kingdom to be found? Where, if not in the body of this society, is the depository of the authority Christ gave? And who should exercise this authority, if not the legally appointed officers of this kingdom? And this kingdom has ever borne the marks its Master bore, the double character of enduring and conquering. Its martyrs, while they seemed to be the victims of a losing cause, were really the heralds of victory, and the Church has bent before the storm only to rise refreshed for new conquests, and its conquerors have dictated terms to it only in turn to receive from the Church conditions which they were compelled to accept. And like its Master, the Church has spoken with authority, and not as the scribe; and through all ages the power and right to retain or remit sins has been held to be inherent, and ever has been ceaselessly and fearlessly exercised.

Now it is against this power claimed by the Christian Church that some of the sharpest darts of criticism are aimed, and unformed Christians see in it the badge of superstition, the rag of Popery, the tyrant efforts of a priesthood to rivet chains on a free people. Mere declamation is of little importance, and all the protests made against a doctrine can be of little value unless they derive a value from the falsity of the position itself. It is more to the purpose to examine into the internal constitution of the Christian kingdom, to search for our credentials, and if we find them to produce them, and fearlessly to claim from Christians whatever may belong to our possession of these credentials.

Before proceeding, it may be as well to point out some things which will prepare the way for our acceptance. The power claimed by human society over its members, is of a kind so similar to that claimed by the Christian Church that it does almost prepare the way for the acceptance of the higher doctrine of the Church, and a consideration of it may modify the feelings with which some people regard it. The power to retain or remit sins is claimed and exercised by society so freely, that it almost startles one to find a similar claim put forward by a spiritual kingdom, as derived from its King and exercised by the authority of its King, exciting any astonishment. It is universally accepted, that a right dwells in a kingdom to punish the violation of its laws by any individual; it is also universally accepted, that society may either punish or forgive the offender. Indeed, the exercise of this power, through the agency of its magistrates, is one of the most important of the functions and duties of kingdoms; while the determination and pertinacity with which we pursue the offender against our laws can hardly escape observation. The thief, or the murderer, or the forger, is tracked to his hiding-place; the officer of justice pursues him across the ocean, and brings him to the bar of judgment: he has offended against the laws of human society, and that society claims the right to remit or to retain, to punish or to forgive. It scarcely needs illustration, yet to make the matter more clear we may dwell on it for a few moments. Offences against the laws of our country are visited with little mercy upon the violator of those laws. The Sepoys rebelled against our government in India, striving, as it seemed to them, to free their country; they were crushed and decimated; and the tale of the suppression of the mutiny is fresh in our memory. They had rebelled against England's rule, and violated England's laws, and the officials of England doled out mercy or judgment as it seemed fit to them, and England ratified the deeds of its officers. Whose sins they remitted, England remitted; and whose sins they retained, England retained; and human society asserted its authority by blowing the poor Sepoys from the cannon's mouth, and hastening them all unshriven into the eternal world; and there seemed nothing strange in this assertion of a country's right to retain or absolve. In all criminal prosecutions which take place, society asserts the same right to absolve or retain; the criminal violates the laws, and is guilty of a crime of a greater or less description, and society rightly enough defends itself, and punishes or absolves the offender, and the judge pronounces the sentence which hurries the criminal to the gallows or sets him at liberty; the judge is the magistrate of human society, and exercises the right claimed by it to remit or retain sins, and none dispute that right. Here is a power exactly analogous to that which it seems to us our Lord entrusted to His

Church, the only difference (though I admit it to be an important difference) being, that one deals with the actions of men as offences against human society, while the other deals with them as offences against human society re-organized by Christ, which possesses and claims to exercise authority in the region where the sources and springs of actions are to be found. Actions, as offences against ordinary society, are capable of punishment or reward, irrespective of the motive power which prompted them. Its sins and its virtues are the deed done: they are sins against society, and are dealt with by the magistrate, whose decisions are ratified by the sovereign. Sins of conscience are sins against God, and are to be dealt with not by the magistrate but by the priest: by the representative of a power given to regenerate human society, to remit or retain sins. We extend into the region of conscience an authority which is constantly exercised in the region of actions. Men say such power is too great to be entrusted to man over his fellows: it is difficult to see force in such an argument, considering the immense influences exercised by society over its members, and the effect that influence has upon our spiritual prospects. The authority which, dealing with conscience, tries to check and reform, is a merciful authority compared with that which blows poor Sepoys from the cannon's mouth, to find or miss in heaven the mercy they had failed to find on earth.

Christianity has been resolved in so many minds into a mere phase of opinion, and the abundant notices contained in the New Testament of our Lord's work in organizing a visible Church, have been so entirely overlooked, that it is very necessary to place much stress upon the authority which our Lord claimed for Himself, and which He gave to the kingdom He was founding;

especially as many of the most important statements of the Scripture are utterly incomprehensible, if we banish the Holy Catholic Church from our creed. Christ claiming to be a King, and organizing by His disciples a visible kingdom in the world, is the burden of the New Testament: while the powers with which He invested the new kingdom all spring out of and result from the authority with which our Lord was Himself invested. He proved the power possessed by the Son of Man to forgive sins when He cured the man sick of the palsy. He invested His kingdom with this power over the consciences of its members, when He said, "Whose soever sins ye remit, they are remitted unto them; and whose soever sins ye retain, they are retained." And He promised to ratify the decisions of His Church when He said, "If he refuse to hear thee, tell it to the Church; if he shall not hear the Church, he shall be to thee as a Gentile or a publican. Verily I say unto you, Whatsoever things ye shall bind on earth, shall be bound in heaven: and whatsoever things ye shall loose on earth, shall be loosed in heaven." Here is the promise of a ratification by Him, our absent King, of the official acts of the Church on earth.

If in His suffering and death our Lord became the Lamb of God, of which the sacrificial lamb was the type, the work of His life, His claims of authority, the teaching of His parables, the training of His Apostles, all set Him forth as fulfilling the prophecies which tell of a king coming to reign, and of a kingdom which should have no end. That wondrous life and death have been long since wrought out, and the suffering and conquering Messiah are blended for ever in our mind in Him who died on Calvary, and who, having become Victor in death, spoke to His Apostles in the language of authority, and said, "Go ye into all the world and preach the Gospel to every creature: he that believeth and is baptized shall be saved, and he that believeth not shall be damned." Christ is our King, and the Catholic Church, with its ever-extending bounds, is the kingdom that shall have no end.

But men object to authority in the region of conscience, and speak of any exercise of it as a tyranny; and it sounds well to talk so. Yet a recognised authority is of the utmost value, not as a tyranny but as an ultimate court of appeal to quiet doubts; and in this respect the authority of Christian dogma has been of immense value, not as a tyrant but as a helper, not as the oppressor of human thought but as its saviour. We know the scepticism embodied in Pilate's question, "What is truth?" and we believe our Lord's assertion that He came to bear witness to the truth. How did He witness, but by supplying authoritatively a few dogmatic truths, round which all human thought might afterward cluster, and by which it should be interpenetrated and ennobled. That the Christian creeds have given fixity to human thought, and definiteness to human faith, it is impossible to doubt; and they have not affected this by crushing human thought; but by the authoritative solution of problems we could not solve, they have freed for the pursuit of other truths efforts which were being wasted in fruitless guesses. Dogma is the vertebra, the backbone of truth; dogma is the nucleus around which all human thoughts may cluster, and gather from it life and strength. In this respect the kingdom of heaven has supplied the shortcomings of the intellectual world; giving us a faith instead of a superstition; dogma, in place of wild guesses; creeds, in the place of uncertain statements. And its value has been and is this, that it speaks with authority, and not as the scribe; it is a voice speaking to the realms of conscience with an authority conscience feels bound to recognise: and authority thus in the realms of conscience has been and is of the highest possible value; and we must admire His knowledge who, seeing the want, so wisely supplied it; authority in the realm of conscience has been the end of strife, and the strife has been ended by a voice which conscience recognises.

There are constant witnesses that the authority possessed by human society needs supplementing by an authority dealing in the regions of conscience. For it is in that region the sources and springs of all our miseries are found. Our Lord pointed to this when He said, "Out of the heart proceed evil thoughts, adulteries, fornications, &c.; these are the things that defile the man." The act is only the crystallized thought; and any true reformation must be accomplished by work done in that region, and society is ever bearing witness to the felt necessity of such dealing. When any great crime has been committed and punishment has been adjudged, we are anxious to justify our own judgment by extorting, if possible, the confession of guilt. But conscience is not amenable to any authority that is only the voice of man; it will only yield to an authority which comes from Him to "whom all hearts are open, all desires are known, and from whom no secrets are hid." To such an authority conscience has yielded up its secrets, and will yield them up; but to any lower claim it never has yielded, and it never will yield. And society has often had to acknowledge its impotence; against the cold north wind of human authority conscience gathers up its cloke, refusing to yield, and sinks the secret deep in that impenetrable abyss into which no human eye shall ever look, and from which no human hand shall ever extract it. But it has been and is different with the authority of Christ's kingdom; men have recognised its right to deal with conscience, and have yielded up their secrets. Constance Kent stood unblanched before a human tribunal, and listened unmoved to the screams of a helpless public opinion; it was not in its power to extract the secret; it was conscience yielding to an authority which it felt bound to recognise which brought the murderer before the bar of human society. It was the Kingdom of Heaven supplementing the imperfect authority of human society, dealing authoritatively in a region beyond the power of human law. And the necessity of some authority to deal with men, if any true reformation is to be accomplished, is obvious in another matter. We are always aiming, as the great object of our preaching, to bring about conviction of sin, and to induce men to accept those responsibilities which, as Christians, they are bound to recognise. And the throes of a convicted conscience are among the most wonderful facts with which the Christian priesthood has to deal. The course of this wonderful change, as described in ordinary dissenting works, is well known; there is the troubled conscience, the awakening to the conviction of sin, the terrors of a broken law, and the peace of a soul which has found forgiveness. This is the stereotyped story, and we who have to do with human souls, are acquainted with the utterly unsatisfactory character of the process. There are some minds whose native force of character enables them to work out this matter to a proper conclusion; but in nine cases out of ten the peace which is called the consciousness of pardon is just the exhaustion that follows an unnatural excitement. It is just in these trying periods of the Christian life that there is felt the necessity of some authoritative guidance, an authority so recognised that the troubled conscience will appeal to it, and for want of which so many strong convictions die away without a true repentance, and without a solid amendment, until at last men are tempted to regard the convictions as themselves worthless.

The Kingdom of Heaven has supplied this need; and though in England this valuable feature of Christ's instructions has been neglected, it is enshrined in the Scripture and asserted in our Prayer-book, and the neglected truth must again be put forward. In the invitation to the Sacrament the scriptural method of proceeding is put forward. Self-examination is urged, but it goes on to say, "If there be any of you, who by this means cannot quiet his own conscience herein, but requireth further comfort or counsel, let him come to me, or to some other discreet and learned minister of God's Word, and open his grief; that by the ministry of God's holy Word he may receive the benefit of absolution, together with ghostly counsel and advice, to the quieting of his conscience, and avoiding of all scruple and doubtfulness." Here is a definite relationship shewn betwixt the priest and the people; and those who have in their times of doubt acted upon it and used it, and have been guided in the paths of a true repentance and received the authoritative absolution, know the comfort that springs from it, and the blessedness of the work which by this scriptural method is accomplished. The executive of a society intrusted with authority has spoken with authority in the region of conscience, and given peace; and instead of that false peace which is the mere quiet of exhaustion, there is the consciousness of true penitence, and the assurance springing from a pardon spoken by one who has authority to speak it, and who therefore speaks with authority, and not as the scribe. So the Kingdom of Heaven supplements the imperfections of human society; and we must admire His knowledge of human society and of its wants who entrusted to His kingdom the needful authority by saying, "Whose soever sins ye remit, they are remitted unto them; and whose soever sins ye retain, they are retained," for so the Victor on His Throne absolves His people.

The absolving power is, then, one among other methods by which our Blessed Lord has supplemented the authority of human society, and given stability to human thought and action; and He has done so, not by tyrannizing in the human intellect or human heart, but by solving for the intellect problems impossible to it, and giving the Church the authority necessary to enable souls to work out their spiritual convictions to a healthy result.

Though not immediately illustrating this subject, we may notice another way in which the Catholic Church presents this same supplemental character. Human society is an unstable thing, wanting any permanent bond of union; it is ever shifting, gathering now round one centre, now round another; now adopting one form of government, and now another; divided at times into the deep antagonisms of clanships, fighting with savage instincts over every trifle. Men grouped themselves in Greece under its petty tyrannies, each standing off from the other and engaged in eternal strife, until the power of Rome stepped in and deprived them of the liberty of mutual slaughter by depriving them of liberty itself, and embracing all the petty states in a province of its world-wide empire. Christ came into the world when Rome, having crushed all beneath her grasp, was commencing her own drift towards dissolution. He came to found a kingdom which should not change; with a few fixed outlines of government, a definite organization constructed for all nations and all times, a bond that would unite men together in one great family. And it has realized the purpose, for it has been, and still is, the permanent in the midst of the unpermanent, the eternal in the midst of change; and possibly now, when the past is strangely breaking up, and in politics people can find no abiding principle, this Catholic Church may form a nucleus round which men may gather to obtain stability in the midst of change, and to escape from the petty rivalries of national strife, in a brotherhood which knows no distinctions, Englishman or American, German or French, but all are one in Christ. Through the changes of the Middle Ages it formed a home of rest; in the changes and doubts of the present time it may prove to be, not the tyrant but the helper of intellect, not the tyrant but the comforter of conscience, not the tyrant but the liberator of nations; and in so far as it shall be the helper of the intellect, the comforter of the conscience, and the liberator of nations, we shall learn to admire the wisdom which speaks with authority, and not as the scribe.

This definiteness in the whole position occupied by the Catholic Church, contrasts remarkably with the indefiniteness which marks ordinary Protestant teaching, rendering it so utterly unsatisfactory to all thoughtful minds. Had the men who led the great evangelical movement fifty years ago grasped the doctrine of the Incarnation and Atonement more completely, that movement would have had a far greater aspect of finality than it now has. But its imperfection is witnessed to by the unstable attitude of those who are trying to make a stand upon it. With no positive line which they can defend, they shift incessantly from pillar to post, accusing others of denying the doctrine of the Incarnation whose only fault is that they see and embrace it with a clearness and entirety which the evangelical party seems utterly unable to attain to; and the clear grasp of Christian truth which Catholics in the Church have reached, must have its weight.

An invisible Church, with invisible gates, containing only invisible people, may suit the fervid souls of sectarians, but can have few attractions to sober Bible-reading Christians. In the ordinary Protestant theory there is a want of definiteness about everything. We are told by it of the blood of sprinkling with which each soul must be washed, but it knows nothing of the way in which that blood is to be applied. We are told of pardon of sin, and the only assurance is to be sought for and found in the pardoned. We are presented with sacraments which have no reality in them, but are at best indifferent substitutes for sermons. In contrast with these most unsatisfactory theories, the Catholic religion presents us with sacraments where the blood of sprinkling may be found, and with pardon conveyed to us by the accredited authorities of Christ's Church. The Catholic religion is all that Protestantism is, but something more; and nowhere is its superiority shewn more clearly than in the exercise of the absolving power. It is beautifully set forth in the absolution pronounced by the executive of the Christian Church at public worship. It is more strikingly seen in the absolution preparatory to the Holy Communion; there the Victor absolves and then sprinkles with His blood. But possibly, no aspect of the absolving power presents the Victor to us in so glorious a manner as that which

He presents to us, when, in the extreme hour of weakness, the penitent trembles on the verge of the eternal world. Strength and weakness then shew by contrast. There is the Victor on His Throne, receiving the homage of the spiritual world, omnipotent, omnipresent; and there is the penitent, the last failing power of life only left, with intellect too feeble to measure the value of his position or to grasp a theory, yet with conscience strong enough to feel the sense of sin; able to perceive the stain, yet unable to use one effort to wash the stain away. The Victor and the penitent then stand in strange contrast. And what does ordinary Protestantism do at such a moment? What does it offer? It appeals to the *feelings* of the penitent; it says, "Do you feel happy?" What! make an appeal to the *feelings* of the dying hour, when the whole mental power is nigh to extinction, and the last feeble flash of life is glimmering in the socket; to look to the feelings of that moment for an assurance, oh, this is the last degrading end of a degrading superstition. Through life the poor soul has been the victim of a mistake, which makes men look to their frames and feelings for the evidence of their spiritual life; and the superstition hangs over their dying hour, making the clouds that darken the soul in its dying agony the proof of a perishing soul, and the fever gleams that flash for a moment in the expiring socket a proof of salvation. Miserable delusion; the last end of a degrading superstition. Instead of bringing strength to weakness, it appeals to weakness for strength; instead of bringing the absolving power and the cleansing blood to the poor penitent, it leaves the poor soul to seek and find them where it may. Contrast this with the Gospel plan. One who has held the faith of Christ, knows in that hour where to look for strength, and Christ, the Victor, knows where true weakness is. The weight of sin is on the penitent's soul, and he may not die with that burden on him; but Christ has said, "Whose soever sins ye remit, they are remitted unto them; and whose soever sins ye retain, they are retained." And the priest of the kingdom that He has founded, of the Church which He purchased with His blood, comes to the dying penitent, an accredited messenger from the Victor on His Throne; the magistrate of the kingdom, comes with the authority Christ gave to His kingdom, and says, "By His authority committed to me, I absolve thee from all thy sins, in the name of the Father, and of the Son, and of the Holy Ghost." He is the officer of that kingdom, to the body of which Christ committed authority over its members, and the poor penitent, hearing these words, remembers that the Victor said, "Whose soever sins ye remit, they are remitted unto them; and whose soever sins ye retain, they are retained," and he has confidence.

Here indeed is ground for assurance; it is pardon and peace spoken as then it needs to be spoken, with authority, and not as by the scribe; and it gives true peace. He comes to loose, and Christ has said "Whatsoever ye shall bind on earth, shall be bound in heaven; and whatsoever ye shall loose on earth, shall be loosed in heaven." He is the officer of a kingdom whose King has promised to ratify the official acts of His kingdom. Here is the messenger of the Victor to speak with authority, and not as the scribe; and when He has thus spoken, and absolved the penitent, the Altar is spread, and the Victor present by His priest to pardon, is, Himself, present in His Sacrament to cleanse and sprinkle with that blood which is drink indeed, and with that body which is meat indeed. Here is the action of a living faith, here is ground for assurance— it is pardon and peace spoken with authority, and it gives true peace: it is strength perfected in weakness: it is the Victor on His Throne absolving the penitent, and men need not wonder if He speaks with authority, and not as the scribe.

I have thus with plainness dealt with this great question, which does so much disturb the minds of men; and I know I have put forward views which will at once seem to some a proof of unfaithfulness. We are told that Englishmen will never accept such teachings; that they will never obey any human authority. I know, or think I know something of my countrymen; I know their impulsiveness, their hatred too of all tyranny; their genuine love of that which seems to them to be truth; but I believe too that amidst all religious differences, they do with heart and soul love Jesus, and that they will readily obey a law or rule which seems to them to express His will; and because I think the thoughts I have put before you do express His will, I do not fear to set them forward, thinking that truth is great and will prevail; and all we ask is that what we have to say shall be fairly and dispassionately weighed. For, what are those among us to do, who believe that what we call the Catholic faith is but imperfectly understood, and that to fulfil the will of Christ a fuller view of Christianity is necessary? Are we to be silent? Are we to shrink back because such thoughts are unpopular? The growth of truth is not in this way served. We must freely and fairly state what we believe to be truth, trusting to the power there is in truth to make its way and gain acceptance; and however unwilling Englishmen may be to accept it, the time may come when greater knowledge and a clearer comprehension of the meaning of Catholic truth shall very much change their thoughts, and make them ready to accept what they now reject. Truth always has to work its way upward from minorities to majorities; all forms of truth have had to do this; and we work on, striving to extend Christ's visible kingdom, and to deepen the character of the Christian faith, feeling that we, like our Master, must bear witness to the truth, and, if need be, suffer loss for its sake; for there is coming a time when all motives and all actions will be searched into and tried by the clear light of the great day of judgment, and an absolution shall be pronounced by the Victor on His Throne, not through another, but by His own lips; and then when the words of pardon are uttered, we, remembering all our short-comings and our many sins, shall wonder that in that form of absolution no mention of sin is made; but that the little good we have contrived to do for Him, exaggerated by the loving soul of Jesus, shall seem to be a reason for our receiving the blessing which His blood alone had purchased. Then in that hour the little we have done or suffered for the cause of truth will seem as nothing, and we shall rejoice that we were permitted to speak in His Name, and to bear witness for that truth; and, Christians, the joy of that hour will more than compensate for any cross we may have to bear now. It may be, and it doubtless will be, that we shall see that our best views of truth were but feeble conceptions of the truth itself; but He who, blinding Himself to the sins done and duties left undone, sees only the little good, and yet says, "Come, ye blessed children of My Father, inherit the kingdom prepared for you from the foundation of the world." That Holy One, who knows how we see through a glass darkly, shall know the boldness which made men speak for that truth, and shall confess us in the great day before men; and we, seeing the Victor upon His Throne, and hearing His blessed words of love, shall rejoice that we had faith to believe and preach His words: "Whose soever sins ye remit, they are remitted unto them; and whose soever sins ye retain, they are retained."

SERMON XI.

The Victor, on His Throne, holding the Keys of Hell and of Death.

ACTS vii. 59.

"Lord Jesus, receive my spirit."

IF we can set ourselves to think what it will be to die, we must feel what a tremendous trial we shall have to pass through at the hour of death. It will be a very sore thing to have to bear the pangs and sufferings of a wasting sickness, to pine away day after day, and at last, all weak, and worn, and feeble, to meet that sharp struggle in which soul and body are parted asunder. And over and above this, we can hardly doubt that for most of us the time when we lie dying will be a time of very great distress for the soul. We must almost expect to be assaulted then by fears, and doubts, and temptations of a peculiar character. If ever the Evil One sets upon us to cut us off from God, he is likely to set upon us then with all his force and craft. He will know that his time is short, and he will try to make sure of our souls before the sand of life is run out. We shall have to do battle with him in a deadly conflict; and so we feel that our last moments in this world will be moments of tremendous trial. We are right. But, my brethren, do we feel that the first moment after death, the first moment in the next world, the first moment when we have closed our eyes on all that we are used to in this world, the first moment when we have opened the eyes of the soul on all that is new, and strange, and unknown—will be more tremendous still? If we do not in some degree realize how amazing and awful that moment will be, we shall hardly see the need of believing in the power that our blessed Lord has to aid the soul which has passed away from the world.

Let me ask you, then, to begin to-night, by trying to master the thought of a soul passing away from this world. And first, to aid you in this, take the case of St. Stephen, whose last dying moments are described in the history from which the text is taken. What do we think of, as we read that story of the first martyr's death, sketched for us by St. Luke with the power as of a painter, so as to call up the whole scene vividly before us? We seem to see, perhaps, the raging crowd gathering in fierceness round their intended victim. With one mad onslaught they rush upon him, and hurl their stones at him. The very violence with which they hurl stone after stone seems to be at once a relief to their pent-up fury, and also to lash them into a fiercer cruelty. And there is St. Stephen in the midst of those who are venting their rage upon him, wherever he turns meeting the glare of their rage, not a friend near to comfort or aid him, mangled and wounded as blow follows blow. And then we hear him call upon our blessed Lord, and we think in wonder of the stedfast faith which made him see and feel how near our blessed Lord was to him. He seems to forget all else,—the cries, the blows, the noise, the fierceness. His gaze, his heart, his soul, is fixed on our blessed Lord, as if he were alone with Him, and so he speaks to Him, and says, "Lord Jesus, receive my spirit." It is, indeed, a wonderful faith, of which we have the history here. It shews us the soul of the suffering disciple leaning on the Lord who had suffered. We see that the secret of strength in all trials lies in appealing to the love and power of the blessed Jesus. In the death-struggle, St. Stephen had faith to hang upon his Lord, and his Lord bore him through the agonies of that hour. This is what we are most likely to think of in reading of the martyr's death. But was this the greatest proof of St. Stephen's faith? Was his greatest trial in this world? Did it not lie beyond the world? The life was nearly crushed out of him. The pains of death were coming thick and fast upon him. But was death the end? What was awaiting him after death? He was entering on the unseen state. All was dim, unknown, untried, before him. He must have felt as if his whole being was giving way, as if there were no ground beneath his feet, as if he were sinking into a fathomless abyss. He was going, but whither? And if he was passing into the world of spirits, would he be safe from all enemies there? We think of his falling asleep, and it soothes us to read the words. We feel that the pelting of the bloody storm of stones ceased at last, and that the spirit of the martyr had left his enemies behind. They had killed the body, and they had no more that they could do. But were there not fiercer enemies that were not left behind? Had Satan and his angels lost all power over that spirit? Could the dying martyr be sure that he should escape from these? And then, once more, if his spirit passed away, to whom would it go? It must return to God Who gave it. It must go before God, meet Him, and give up its account to Him. It is such thoughts as these which add so wonderful a power and force to those words, "'Lord Jesus, receive my spirit.' I know not where I go. All nature seems to open out into vast untried depths beneath me. Take me, hold me in Thine everlasting arms; I am safe with Thee. I know not who may attack me, how the powers of evil may gather against me; take me, guard me. I know not how to meet the judgment. I know only that I have been dear to Thee in this life. Thou hast loved me, died for me, kept me. Take me now; to Thee do I commit my cause. 'Lord Jesus, receive my spirit.'" Here is indeed a strange, calm faith in the power of our blessed Lord to keep and bless the soul in that unseen world. One who could speak thus must have felt that our Lord had conquered in that world, as in this, and emptied it of its horrors.

He looked, as it were, through the mist and darkness that was gathering round him; he pierced with the steady gaze of his mind through the veil that was drawn between him and the state on which he was entering, and there he saw his Lord waiting and ready for him. Or rather, with a surer faith, though he did not *see*, he *felt* certain that our Lord was King in that realm of the departed, and he was ready to pass into it because he knew that our Lord had power to keep and uphold him there. Ah, brethren, perhaps we shall never know the full force of those calm words of St. Stephen's till we are on the edge of that unseen world ourselves.

And now the next thing which I would ask you to do is to try and bring before you the peculiar trial of passing into the unseen world. We can only try to imagine it, but it may be of use to us to make the effort.

Take, then, such points as these :—

1. The moment will come when your soul will leave the body. There are two moments before you, in the first of which you will be still in this world, in the second of which you will have passed out of the world. This

we all know well. But do we know no more than this? *We* cannot see into the world of spirits, but our Lord can. All souls live under His eye, whether they are in the body or out of the body. And He has given us the history of two departed souls. He tells us how the soul of the beggar Lazarus, immediately after death, was carried by the angels to Abraham's bosom, and there was soothed and comforted after the sufferings of the world were passed. He tells us also of the wretched soul of the rich man, and of the torments into which it was cast. Between the two a great gulf was fixed. One was in misery, the other was in peace. Their state was settled, as it could only be settled, by some secret judgment of God. Our Lord speaks of both these men as living still in the spirit, thinking, feeling, using their powers and energies. One knew the comforts with which he was visited, the other knew the torments to which he had been condemned. And both had memories of the past. One could look back upon the *sorrows* from which he had been released, the other could look back upon the *sins* which had brought him to "the place of torment."

We have the histories of two other souls given to us in Holy Scripture. We are told of the wretched Judas in words pregnant with a terrible meaning, that "he went to his own place." We are told of the penitent thief that it was promised to him that on the very day on which he died he should be with our blessed Lord in Paradise. And so we may gather what will be the case with each of us when we die. Each of us will go to his own place, as God shall appoint, and fix that place for us. And if this be so, then one by one we shall have to pass under the sentence of God.

My brethren, try and think what the effect upon us

of that one moment will be! Will it not seem like an age? How will all our past days and hours be crowded into that moment, as we live them over again in memory,—no, not in memory, but in one clear, vivid present! And then, bear in mind that all outward things will be shut out from us. The sights and sounds of this world will have been left behind. In our present state a thousand things carry away our thoughts from ourselves. We are always forgetting ourselves in what others do or say. The mind wanders off to this thing or to that, and finds relief in change. But in that moment the whole powers of the mind will be turned inwards, and bent upon itself. There will be not a word, not a whisper, not a sound, not a motion to distract it from itself. It will be alone. And yet again, in one sense, it will not be alone. The soul will feel that it is before God! Yes! *we*—let us speak plainly, that we may realize what it is that we shall have to pass through,—*we* shall feel that we are alone with God. We shall feel that we are under His gaze, His piercing, searching gaze, and that He is reading us through and through. He will see us; we shall feel that He sees us. And in some sense we shall see Him. We shall probably know what He is, as we have never known it before. We shall have such a notion as a creature may have of His pure, spotless holiness, of His bright and glorious perfection. And with this what must come but a sense of the abomination of sin in His sight?

We have heard that "He is of purer eyes than to behold iniquity,"—we shall know *then* what this means, when we are alone with Him, shut in from all created beings, face to face with His purity, in the moment when He has required our souls of us. What will our life look like to *Him* then? And what will it look like to *us?* There may be a hundred faults which we have made ourselves easy about, because they are so *common,* or because it is the way of the world to *excuse* them. Alas! such excuses will shrivel like tow before the fire, when we have to face the consuming brightness of the holiness of God. What are those faults to *Him?* What will He think of the ease, the carelessness, the forgetfulness of Him, the ingratitude with which we have committed them, and committed them again and again? What shall we think of having grieved Him by each separate sin that we once made so light of? We shall see clearly then what we know even now, if we would stop to consider it, that by each bad act which we do we scorn the love of God, by each bad word which we speak we affront His listening ear, by each bad thought which we indulge we thrust our foulness upon His sorrowing eye. What shall we feel when all this comes vividly before us? And then, add to this what will be perhaps the most overwhelming feeling, the remembrance of all that God has been to us, and all that He has done for us. Imagine this bursting upon us; imagine God revealing to us all the whole history of His acts of love towards us, so that we see at a glance every grace that He has ever given us, all His calls, and warnings, and invitations, His lessons, His drawing of our hearts to Him, His devices and plans to win us, His many thousand aids bestowed on us; and so our awakening up to all that we might have been, and to all that we are; our seeing clearly all His vast love, and all our ingenuity in thwarting His purposes. Ah! my brethren, think deeply of all this, and you will see that **the moment in which the soul passes before God is the most tremendous of all moments.**

2. But have we any reason to suppose that what the soul feels and knows about itself in that moment, will pass away and be forgotten? Surely all that we know about our own powers, all that we know about the love of God, would lead us to believe that the memory of that meeting with God would live on in the soul, and work most powerfully upon it for good. Probably we ourselves, even now, rarely or never forget altogether what has settled down in our minds. At any rate, it is strange to see how a slight circumstance will bring before us things which have happened long years ago in all their most minute particularity, when we fancied that we had forgotten them. And certainly when God calls, and warns, and teaches us, He does not mean that we should forget His revelations. It is part of our misery in this world that so many things for a while cover over, and hide what He writes with His finger on the soul, as dust gathers over an inscription until it cannot be read. In the unseen world there will be nothing to turn away the mind from the thought of God and of itself. Surely, then, the vision of God will live on in us. The sight which we have of Him in that moment, when we pass beyond all the distractions of the world, to see nothing but Him, will be stamped upon our spirits. And the sight which we had of ourselves, in our own true, real character, as shewn to us by God, with all our past sins, faults, failings, imperfections, and corruptions, will remain fixed there also.

3. But will not this be torture, and misery, and wretchedness to the soul? No: for it will not be alone in that state of the departed. Our blessed Lord will be present there. He has taken possession of that realm; He has made it His own; He blessed it with His visible presence when He descended into hell; He

claimed for His own soul as man the guardian care, the comforts, the support, the presence of God with the departed, when He said, "Father! into Thy hands I commend My Spirit." He assured the same protection and the same comforts of God, of which He tasted Himself, to us who are the members of His Body; for all which He took for Himself as the head, He took that we might share it with Him. He has claimed as part of His kingdom that abode of souls, for, when the penitent thief asked to be remembered by Him when He came into His kingdom, He answered, "To-day shalt thou be with Me in Paradise:"—this very day thou shalt know what it is to be with Me, to feel Me near thee, guiding, teaching, comforting, assuring thee that thou art Mine for ever. There is a mysterious passage which seems to tell us how He Himself bore revelations of His love and mercy to the spirits of those in that unseen world,—"The Gospel was preached to them that are dead." And so doubtless He reveals Himself to them still. The manner of His presence with the departed may not be the same as when His soul was amongst them, while His body lay in the grave, but we need not doubt that He is there present still. The manner of His presence with us on earth is different from what it was when He was seen by men in the flesh, but we know that He is with us even to the end of the world. And so we cannot but believe that He is still present with the departed, and puts forth His power and love to bless them. Nay, He seems Himself to claim this power over the place of departed spirits as part of the special fruits of His own victory over death, when He says, "I am He that liveth, and was dead, and behold I am alive for evermore, and have the keys of hell and of death."

Pause here, then, and imagine what must be the effect of that presence of our blessed Lord upon the departed spirits. As the sight of their past sin broods upon their minds, how may we believe that He makes them hate and abhor that old pollution! As the knowledge of the purity of God sinks down into their being, and its beauty and fairness grows upon them, how must He make that knowledge work in them, till they crave and long to be made more and more pure themselves! As the memory of all God's wondrous love to them melts, and entrances them more and more, how must our Lord give force to that memory, and so quicken their longings to be brought nearer and nearer to the very presence of God unveiled in heaven! We may well trust that in His conquering power our Lord will thus overrule all that might hurt the soul, and turn it into a gain. We may perhaps even venture to use His words by the Prophet Hosea as though they were spoken to the spirit before the full and final triumph of the resurrection hour has arrived: "I will ransom thee from the power of the grave; I will redeem thee from death. O death, I will be thy plagues; O grave, I will be thy destruction."

4. But this is not all which we may say of the power of our Lord in the world of departed spirits. There must be blessings and gifts which He bestows upon the spirits there, far beyond those which He gives here. So great are those blessings, that St. Paul longed to depart and be with our Lord. The Apostle had seen our Lord in glory while he was in this world. He had had abundant revelations from Him. He had heard His voice. He had felt the strength of our Lord working in him so powerfully that it overcame his own weakness. He had even learnt to rejoice in suffering.

because it gave an opportunity for our Lord to shew how near He was to His disciple. So closely was he bound to our Lord, that he says that he lived by the life of Christ. And yet he felt that after death our blessed Lord would be nearer to him, and he would be nearer to our Lord. There was greater joy and happiness in store for him, when he should be set free from this world. Can we not guess how this would be? Think only how all that is in the world comes between us and our Lord, and draws away our hearts from Him, or threatens to fill our hearts and leave no room for Him to work in them. The grace of Christ works within us. What should we be if it did not? But we live in the midst of coldness and carelessness, which check the love of God in us. The frost of the world chills the soul, and keeps it from putting out in full beauty the fruits of the Spirit. What, again, then, must it be to depart from this world, and to be taken into that nearer presence of our Lord, where He shall foster and cherish the soul, while there will be nothing to interfere any longer with His loving influence over it! There must be times in the lives of nearly all of us, when the sore struggle against temptation, or the sharpness of the conflict in standing out against the bad example of those around us, or the weight of the sorrows of life, or the very comforts of grace with which God blesses us now, make us turn our longing eyes towards the peace, and calm, and safety of Paradise. We are ready to cry out with St. Paul, "I have a desire to depart, and to be with Christ;" "O that I had wings like a dove, for then would I flee away" from the strife, and din, and stress, and weariness of the battle of life, "and be at rest." Even before our appointed hour has come, when the storm of a great trial is pelting ceaselessly upon us, we are tempted to cry out, "'Lord Jesus, receive my spirit:'—oh! take me, and gather me unto Thyself. 'Hide me secretly in Thy Tabernacle from the strife of tongues!'" So do we long to be sheltered, and soothed by Him.

And will not this very longing of our hearts suggest to us how He will deal with the faithful soul when He has at last taken it to Himself? How will He calm, and soothe, and refresh it after the trials of life! "Blessed are the dead which die in the Lord. Yea! saith the Spirit, for they rest from their labours." When the souls under the Altar cry out, there are given unto them white robes. How full of promise to all that have suffered in faith and patience in this life are those words which our Lord spoke of the soul of Lazarus: "Now, he is comforted!" He received evil things in this life, but now he is comforted. How do they seem to tell us of our blessed Lord watching those who love Him, in their sorrows and sufferings here below, and waiting to bless them, when the trial hour shall be past! Surely His eye marks every pang we bear for His sake, every struggle we make to do His will, every faintness of our worn spirit as the battle bears down hard upon us. He marks, He remembers them all;—and He will comfort us in His own good time. As a mother takes up her child after a night of agony, and folds it in her arms, and soothes it—so our Lord will take up our spirits, when the sufferings of life are past, and calm, and still every throb of anguish in them. Yes! when He calls us from this world it is as though He spoke His own old words that have cheered us so often, only with a deeper, fuller meaning,—"Come unto Me, all ye that labour and are heavy laden, and I will give you rest."

But even rest and calm are not all that we shall gain from being with Him in that unseen world. How could it be? If our blessed Lord is in some sense nearer to the soul there, even than He is here,—so that St. Stephen could ask Him to take his spirit to Himself, and St. Paul could speak of his being more with Christ after he had departed from this world,—then that presence must help to change, to influence, to purify the soul. What must it be to be brought in any way nearer to Him, to know more of Him, of His wisdom, of His holiness, of His purity, of His tenderness, of His love! We cannot live in constant intercourse with a wise and holy friend, without feeling the force of his character and example. He lifts and raises us out of and above ourselves. His presence keeps down what is evil in us: it draws out all the better parts of our nature. How much more will the presence of our Lord so act upon us! Even in this world St. Paul teaches us that by "beholding as in a glass the glory of the Lord, we are changed into the same image from glory to glory." If this is so here, where there is still so much to distract, who can venture even to guess what may be the power of the presence of Christ to work upon the soul in that world when it is gathered into a place of secluded secrecy, from which every evil influence is banished? How will our Lord Himself, who began the good work in the soul, perform and carry it on until His day! How will He make it more and more like Himself in love, and purity, and perfection!

These, then, are the victories of our blessed Lord in the valley of the shadow of death. He has made that place of separation a safe and calm resting-place, and a school of preparation for the glory of heaven[a]. He

---

[a] Dr. Newman, in a sermon preached at Oxford, describes the state of the departed as "a school-time of contemplation, as this world is a disci-

has received the souls that enter Paradise to Himself. They are in His hand. They are "absent from the body" and "present with the Lord." He guards, guides, and sustains them. He has turned their sad memories of the past into blessed and healing lessons of the hateful nature of sin. He quickens their longings after God, and meets those longings with fresh consolations. He soothes them after the trials of life. He visits them, and blesses them with His presence, and so leads them onwards to the day of their perfected joy at the resurrection. And then He shews Himself to be the Lord both of the dead and of the living. On Him all souls hang, in the body or out of the body. He is the strength, and hope, and life of all.

And now, dear brethren, one great lesson rises out of all that has been said. If God has given us but little clear knowledge of that state of the departed, if we have been obliged to guess at what passes in that state, and are not able to speak with absolute certainty, one thing, at least, is clear and certain,—every hope of the soul as it passes from the body centres in our blessed Lord. If, therefore, He is to be our hope and stay after death, He must be our hope and stay now. We must live in close, earnest, true communion with Him. We must live with Him as our friend, our guide, our heart's inmost life. If we wish to feel that we can commit ourselves to Him, and lean upon Him, when our spirits shall have to venture forth at His call into the dim, uncertain, untried world beyond the grave, then we must familiarize ourselves now with His love, His power, His

pline of active service." A Lutheran writer, Martensen, speaks of the same state as "a kingdom of calm thought, and self-fathoming, of remembrance." He calls it "that cloister-like, that monastic, or conventual world." The similarity of thought between these two writers is very remarkable.

gifts, His might. If we hope to say with the calm, undoubting trust of St. Stephen, at that last moment, "Lord Jesus, receive my spirit;" then we must learn such trust beforehand by commending our spirits to Him now. Aim at this, then. Dwell on the greatness of that love which made our Lord die for us. Dwell on that thought during this Lent, when your sins rise up against you, and accuse you. See how He died for us while we were yet sinners. So when you have to go, all sinful as you are, to find your sins coming back upon your mind in that tremendous moment, when you come to appear before the presence of God, you will have learnt to lean on the atoning power of the Cross of your Lord. Let it be often your prayer now, "Lord Jesus, receive my spirit." "Stained as my soul is, take it, count it as Thine own, cleanse it, offer it to God to be accepted through Thee." Make the same prayer, the same offering of yourselves to your Lord in all the dangers of life. As any fierce temptation bears up against you, fly to Him for shelter and safety, with the words, "'Lord Jesus, receive my spirit;'—keep it, shield it, hold it, 'lest it be torn away from Thee.'" As the hosts of the Evil One assault you, lift up the same cry for help. In acts of faith yield up your souls to the Lord. In acts of self-denial and self-sacrifice separate your souls from all else that may interfere with your love for Him, and give to Him, to Him only, the right over them. In acts of love, choose Him, bind yourselves to Him, fasten your affections on Him. In acts of pain and suffering, lay yourselves out, as it were, to be nailed to the Cross by Him, and leave yourselves in His hands. Above all, in acts of communion offer up your souls to Him, ask Him to come and take possession of them. "Lord Jesus, receive my spirit;" "make it Thine own, work in it, bind it to Thyself, unite it, make it one with Thee." So you will find out more and more what He can do, what He can be to the soul. As you live with Him you will be able to die with Him. As all through life you will have found His love come out the more as the trial was the greater, so in that most tremendous trial, when you are on the borders of the unseen world, you will look for a greater love still. You will feel, " He has been there in that world before me ; He is there in power now : He has the keys of hell and of death ; I am not going out of the borders of His kingdom, nor where His love cannot bless :—no, but nearer, nearer to Him :—' Lord Jesus, receive my spirit :' 'though I walk through the valley of the shadow of death, I will fear no evil ; for Thou art with me.' 'I know whom I have believed, and am persuaded that He is able to keep that which I have committed unto Him against that day.'"

SERMON XII.

The Victor, on His Throne, delivering up the Kingdom.

---

1 COR. xv. 28.

"And when all things shall be subdued unto Him, then shall the Son also Himself be subject unto Him that put all things under Him, that God may be all in all."

IN the course of sermons which have been delivered here during this Lenten season, you have had presented to you the Person and the work of Christ as the Victor in the conflict of the Church with evil. It falls to my lot this evening to wind up the series. I have to speak to you,—though not without a deep sense of my own insufficiency for the handling of so great a subject—I have to speak of the termination of the conflict, and of the delivering up of the Kingdom by the Victor. The passage which I have just read to you will furnish my theme. But in order to a right understanding of it, it will be first necessary to take a brief review of the Apostle's argument in the context.

He is reproving certain amongst the Christians at Corinth, who professed indeed to be believers in Christ, but who denied that there was any resurrection of the dead. And he begins by enumerating the leading facts of the Gospel which he had delivered to them. The words seem, as has been often noticed, to assume the form of an elementary Creed. "I delivered unto you," he says, "first of all, that which I also received, how that Christ died for our sins, according to the Scriptures; and that He was buried, and that He rose again (or rather has risen again and now lives [a]) the third day, according to the Scriptures." He then rapidly accumulates some well-known evidences of Christ's resurrection, not failing to add to them the vision vouchsafed to himself, when he was on his way to Damascus; and so concludes this historical summary by affirming that the resurrection of Christ was the one great central truth of which they, the Apostles, were witnesses, the substance of their preaching, and the ground of their faith.

This, then, being the foundation of his great argument, St. Paul proceeds to shew that there is such a close connection between the fact of Christ's resurrection and the general resurrection, that he who refuses to accept the one, cannot believe in the other. Admit that Christ is risen, and as a necessary consequence you are committed to the belief in a resurrection; deny that there is a resurrection of the dead, and you must be prepared to deny that Christ now lives. If it is a true proposition that Christ is risen from the dead, then the correlative must be true, that there is a resurrection. To those who accept such evidence as carries conviction in ordinary cases, there can be no question that Jesus rose, and now lives again; and faith in that fact involves faith in a general resurrection. But how? it may be asked. Let it be granted, you will say, that there may have been an exercise of Divine power in the resurrection of Christ from the dead; how does it follow from hence that all mankind shall be raised?

[a] The perfect ἐγήγερται expresses this.

Well, to begin with, it shews that a resurrection is at least possible. You cannot dismiss the idea of a resurrection as absurd, so long as we can exhibit to you one clear instance of a victory over the grave. The greatness of Divine power is manifested to us in many different ways. We see it in the heavens above. The variety of organization in "celestial bodies" is itself a proof of the possibility of future combinations, infinitely exceeding our present conceptions. We see it in the earth beneath, in the mysterious changes of "bodies terrestrial." We see it in the seed, which continually propagates itself by dying; (for "that which thou sowest is not quickened except it die;") and which thus shews how death is the gate of life, and how identity may be preserved in different combinations, and under new forms. We need not, then, be deterred by any philosophical difficulties from accepting the doctrine of the resurrection. We know that all things were formed at first out of nothing, and that the Divine Will was the sole origin and essence of creation. Is it a greater demand upon my faith to believe that what now exists may be restored to its own body, than to believe in the original creation of matter out of nothing?

But St. Paul's argument does not rest here. He goes on to shew that the resurrection of Christ proves not only the possibility, but the necessity of the general resurrection. Our Lord did not rise merely as an example of a resurrection, but as the great Head and Representative of redeemed humanity. He is "the firstfruits of them that slept," "the first-begotten of the dead." "For as in Adam all die, even so in Christ shall all be made alive." He holds the same relation to the new creation that Adam does to the old. As

Adam was the bringer in of death, so is He the bringer in of life. As from the first Adam death was propagated to the whole human race; so from the Second Adam is life transmitted to all. And therefore His resurrection is not merely an instance of the possibility of the resurrection; it has a vital force, influential upon all mankind, to raise them from their graves. It is the commencement of a prolonged fact, ending in the resurrection of all mankind. It is through the first man that we have derived mortality; it is through the Second that we drink at the fountains of immortality. It is the purpose and appointment of God that the power of evil shall at length be crushed, that the effects of the Fall shall be completely done away, and that all things shall again be brought into subjection to their rightful Lord. For this purpose the Eternal Son became Incarnate, assuming to His Divine Person the mortal nature of man. How the mystery of the Holy Incarnation was accomplished, we know not. We only know the fact. The mode of the fact is hidden from us. "The Word was made Flesh, and tabernacled amongst us." He did not take any particular person into union with Himself. But He took our flesh, our nature, in its very first original element. From the moment of the "overshadowing" of the Holy Ghost, and of the miraculous conception in the womb of the Blessed Virgin, the Godhead and the Manhood were united in the Person of Christ, never to be separated. From that instant He who had existed before from all eternity as the Second Person of the Holy Trinity, began to exist in habit of our flesh; so that thenceforth He has existed in a twofold substance. Thenceforth the Deity and the Humanity have been united in the Person of Jesus, never to be severed. In all the changes of His earthly condition the Deity has been with Him. It has never forsaken Him, not even in death. The Deity was alike with His Soul in Paradise, and with His Body in the grave [b]. It was the God-Man who rose from the dead, the God-Man who ascended. It is the God-Man who now reigns in heaven as Mediator, "from henceforth expecting until His enemies be made His footstool." And then, when all things shall have been subdued unto Him, and when "He shall have put down all rule, and all authority and power," then shall He deliver up the Kingdom to God, even the Father; and then shall the Son also Himself be subject unto Him that put all things under Him; that God, the Father, the Son, and the Holy Ghost, may be all in all.

But how, it will now be asked, can this prophetic announcement of the Apostle be consistent with those passages which speak of the absolute essential Divinity of the Son, and of His consequent co-equality with the Father, and of the perpetuity of His kingdom?

In order to answer these questions, it will be necessary to consider with reverence and humility, though somewhat more in detail, the mystery of the Person of the Son of God, and the purposes for which He now sits on His mediatorial throne.

We know that there is but one God. But in this Unity we are taught "to acknowledge the glory of the eternal Trinity;" the Father, "made of none, neither created nor begotten;" the Son, "begotten from everlasting of the Father;" and the Holy Spirit, proceeding

---

[b] "Even when His soul forsook the tabernacle of His body, His Deity forsook neither body nor soul. If it had, then could we not truly hold, either that the Person of Christ was buried, or that the Person of Christ did raise up Himself from the dead."—*Hooker*, bk. v. § 52.

eternally from both. Each Person by Himself is God, alike Eternal, Omnipresent, Omnipotent, Omniscient. But in this Divine Mystery there is an order: the Father is not of the Son; but the Son is of the Father. The Father is the ἀρχή, the fountain, the original, of the Godhead[c]. The Son of God, as the Only-begotten of the Father, shares His essence, His attributes, His perfections; derived naturally, and not of grace; eternally, and not in time. He is "God of God, Light of Light, Very God of Very God." He is co-enthroned with the Father. He teaches us that "what things soever the Father doeth, these also doeth the Son likewise[d]." The Father "raiseth up the dead, and quickeneth them; even so the Son quickeneth whom He will[e]." All things that the Father hath are His: the authority of the Only-begotten Son is exactly measured by that of Him that begat Him[f].

But at the same time He is a Son; the relation between an earthly father and an earthly son, expressing as nearly as our finite conceptions can grasp it, the relation which subsists between the Divine Father and the Divine Son. There is absolute identity of nature: He is of one substance with the Father. There is also the obedience of the Son: "As becomes a Son and a Divine Person," says St. Chrysostom, "so He obeys; not humanly, but as one acting freely, and having all authority[g]." As such He is represented to us as the Divine Messenger, coming forth from the Father, and taking upon Him that ministry of grace, appointed for Him in the counsels of eternity, both when He ap-

[c] "Pater est principium totius Divinitatis, quia Ipse a nullo est. Non enim habet de quo procedat; sed ab Eo et Filius est genitus, et Spiritus Sanctus procedit."—*Aug. de Trin.*, lib. iv. c. 40.
[d] John v. 19. [e] Ib. 21. [f] St. Chrysostom. [g] Ib., *in loc.*

peared to patriarchs and saints under the Old dispensation, and also under the New, when, having assumed man into the unity of His Person, He conversed with man upon the earth.

As the Son of God, He thought it not robbery to be equal with God. It was His right, His natural right from all eternity, incapable of any change whether of addition or of diminution. Therefore the Incarnation made no difference in His Divine Nature. It is the essential property of Deity that He never changes. He cannot rule at one time and serve at another. "The Incarnation," says Leo, "added nothing to the majesty of the Son of God, and took nothing from it [h]." But if the Divine Nature of the Son is thus unchangeable; as Man, He became subject to the laws and developments of man's nature. That nature, formed of the very substance of the Blessed Virgin, passed through the gradual stages of growth and stature, and of wisdom and favour with God. Moreover we must believe that this human nature in the Person of Christ, by virtue of its union with the Godhead, was either enlarged or restrained as the economy of our redemption required. It was not that the properties of the one nature were infused into the other. But nevertheless, while this wonderful union could add nothing to the higher nature, it did add perfection to the weaker. His human soul could not but be conscious of all things which God works, and yet without possessing that infinite knowledge which belonged to Him as God. His body also received the influences of Deity proportioned to His own counsels and purposes. It was indeed "without spot of sin," though made "in the likeness of sinful flesh;" and

[h] "Majestati Filii Dei corporea nativitas nihil contulit, nihil abstulit."
—*Leo de Nativ.*, Serm. viii.

therefore not exempt from the consequences of sin, (such as sorrow, and weariness, and pain, and death,) until after His resurrection.

What that glorious Body may be now, it is beyond the power of man to conceive. These two inferences only would I draw from what has been so far stated; (1) First, that nothing belonging to the Person of Christ which is created, and therefore limited, can be everywhere present. The Man, Christ Jesus, is now in heaven by a local presence, in that special nearness to God which is described as His "Right Hand;" from whence He shall come at the last day in the same substance of flesh that He carried thither. As God, indeed, He is at the same time everywhere present, and therefore carries everywhere the influence of that Humanity which is inseparably united with the Deity[1]. But "we must be careful lest, while we maintain the glorious Deity of Him who is Man, we deprive Him of the true bodily substance of Man[k]." This first; then (2) secondly, so intimate, so awfully mysterious is the hypostatic union, that I earnestly deprecate any attempts to sketch the life of our Blessed Lord in its human aspect only. He is a twofold sign, from the depth beneath and from the height above; a Child from the earth beneath, a Son from the heaven above. The Divinity and the Humanity in the Person of Christ, God has joined them; and let no man put them asunder. The contemplation

---

[1] "For His Body, being a part of that nature which whole nature is presently joined unto Deity; wheresoever Deity is, it followeth that His bodily substance hath everywhere a presence of true conjunction with Deity. And forasmuch as it is, by virtue of that conjunction made the body of the Son of God, by whom also it was made a sacrifice for the sins of the whole world, this giveth it a presence of force and efficacy throughout all generations of men."—*Hooker*, bk. v. § 55.

[k] Aug., Ep. 187, c. iii., quoted by Hooker.

of the Human Nature out of the light of the Divine may present us with a character, beautiful indeed, and full of grace. But nevertheless such a view can hardly fail to be too earthly and sensuous, below the dignity of Him who is "perfect God" as well as "perfect Man."

With these views of the Person of Christ, let us now consider the purposes for which He reigns. We know that after His triumph over death, the Victor was exalted to His throne, and there was a Name given Him which is "above every name." We know further that this exaltation is the reward of His humiliation. God now glorifies in heaven that nature which yielded Him obedience on earth; and has raised the Mediator as the Son of Man to the super-eminence of power. The expressions which describe His exaltation seem to mount as high as is possible for imagination to reach. He is placed "far above all principality, and power, and might, and dominion, and every name that is named, not only in this world, but also in that which is to come." God has put all things under His feet, leaving nothing, Deity alone excepted, which is not put under Him. But this vast authority is given to Him for a special purpose. It is that He may subdue all things to Himself. And when that end is accomplished, then will He yield up the Sceptre, there being no longer any enemies to subdue. So that the Kingdom is no sooner won, than it is laid at the feet of the Father, as the crowning act of redemption, the completion of that obedience which He manifested in His Incarnation and His Death.

But we must consider this subjection of the Son not merely as an individual act, but, (as the Apostle's argument throughout would lead us to regard it,) as the act of the great Head and Representative of human nature. Now a very slight examination of the passage will,

I think, shew us that the "delivering up of the Kingdom" and the "subjection of the Son" both refer to the same event, and are, in fact, only different modes of expressing the same thing. What, then, is this Kingdom which is at the end to be delivered up to the Father? and how is this event connected with the subjection of the Son? In order to answer this question, we must bear in mind that the dominion of Christ is twofold, whether we consider it in reference to Him who reigns, or with regard to its own nature.

As the Son of God, the Creator of the world, He is Lord of all, holding in His own right the supreme dominion of the world. But as the Son of Man, He has been invested with power over all things—a power partly conferred upon Him while upon earth, but fully conveyed to Him when He was set at "God's own right hand in heavenly places." Now this power has been given to Him as a reward of His obedience. It was because He became obedient unto death, even the death of the Cross, that God has highly exalted Him, and given Him "to be the Head over all things to the Church, which is His Body, the fulness of Him that filleth all in all."

We thus see that the dominion which Christ has acquired, as Man, is twofold. The one universal and absolute, by virtue of which He will reign till all things are put under Him; the other, limited, a kingdom of appropriation[1], consisting of those who become "willing in the day of His power," and yield themselves to His service by a voluntary obedience.

Now it is in this acquired sovereignty of Christ as Man that we are to look for an explanation of the expressions, "the delivering up of the Kingdom," and "the

---

[1] Κατὰ οἰκείωσιν.—St. Chrysostom.

subjection of the Son." A part of this sovereignty has been given for a definite purpose; and when that purpose is accomplished, when all enemies shall have been put under His feet, then will He retire from the victorious conflict, and, as Man, resign His commission, that the Humanity may be subject to the Divinity.

But He reigns not merely that He may crush His enemies, but that He may bring many sons to glory, and that, too, by the same pathway of obedience and of suffering which He has trodden. The world was lost by disobedience, and it is the will of God that it should be saved by obedience. "Lo! I come to do Thy will, O God;" this is the essence of the Redeemer's work, the very genius of His kingdom. It was the perfect, undeviating obedience, both active and passive, of the Son to the Father; it was His spotless life, terminating in the awful sacrifice of atonement on Calvary, which constituted the offering well pleasing to God. It is by this that the victory over Sin and Death has been obtained. But Christ, as we have seen, is one with His redeemed. It is from Him, as the Head of humanity, that the destruction of evil has taken its beginning. And now He is exalted to His mediatorial Throne, that He may complete His glorious conquest. He reigns that every opposing power may be put down, and that He may gather together again in one all things unto Himself, thus restoring harmony throughout God's Universe. But especially that He may bring to glory those whom He has redeemed with His most precious blood, that they may reign with Him for ever. But this cannot be until the whole Body of the Church is subject to God; it cannot be until Sin and Satan shall have been subdued, and the last enemy destroyed. But when the whole body of the Church shall have been set free from sin, then will the subjection of the Body be complete. But Christ is the Head of the Body; hence the subjection of the Body may truly be said to be the subjection of the Son, seeing that the Son is the Head of the Body[m]. Christ is now building up and perfecting a kingdom, which is His Church, His mystical Body, sacramentally and by faith united to Him. This Body is not yet complete, either in numbers or in perfection. The great work is now going on. Each faithful one, by the help of the indwelling Spirit, is gradually overcoming evil, gradually becoming more and more conformed to Christ's image. But there is yet more of suffering to be endured, ere "that which is behind of the afflictions of Christ" is filled up; and every true Christian in every age, by his submission to God in obedience and suffering, is supplying that which is still lacking for the sake of Christ's Body. Not a pang, not a tear is in vain: all is helping forward the great object, complete subjection to God, in the noble freedom of a voluntary obedience. At length the end will come, when the increase and perfection of the Body shall have reached its full measure, and nothing more shall be wanting; all having "come unto a perfect man, unto the measure of the stature of the fulness of Christ." There is something amazingly grand in this view. We see Him now upon the Throne of His omnipotent power. We see Him, the conquering Messiah, with a Name written upon His vesture and upon His thigh, " King of Kings, and Lord of Lords." We see Him, gradually it may seem, according to human estimate, but nevertheless surely, working out the purposes of redemption; gradually gathering in

---

[m] See Greg. Nyssen, Homily on this text.

His own, and drawing unto Himself more and more of that which had been lost by transgression. Subjection again to God; this is the object for which He now reigns. That millions on millions of conscious beings may be brought, through His power, into harmony with God, carried safely through death, and saved for ever; for this object has He been made "Lord both of the dead and of the living." And this can only be attained by union with Himself, who, as God, is ever one with the Father, and as Man has become one with us, that we through Him might become one with God. He is now the only way of access; touching the finite with the hand of His Humanity, and with the hand of His Divinity reaching to the infinite. And thus He is ever drawing to Himself His willing people. The ages as they roll onwards are ever recording new victories over the powers of darkness, the resistance of the world, the weakness of the flesh. Then will come the end, when He, the Pattern Man, the Head of the regenerate race, shall give a visible demonstration of His subjection; and, in proof of His mighty work being accomplished, shall present His own homage as Head of the Body, and, as it were, in the name of the Body, to the Father. And this is the completion of the mediatorial work; the prolonged rebellion closed; the strife of ages hushed for evermore; the Church, the Bride of Christ, presented in her glorious apparel; the Sceptre passed by the Mediator into that Light to which no man may approach; the Victor rendering as Man, and, at the same time, receiving as God, the universal homage of created things.

Not that Christ will then cease to reign. This expression, "the delivering up of the Kingdom," says St. Chrysostom, "must be taken in a sense becoming Deity. If

taken in any other sense it would imply two absurdities;
1. that He would not afterwards retain it, and, 2. that the
Father had not before possessed itⁿ." He will never resign His dominion over those whom He has purchased
with His own blood. "For His kingdom lasteth, and
grows not faint until He has accomplished all things;
and when He has accomplished all things, then it lasts
much more; for of His kingdom there is no end^o." Our
life is bound up with His life. It is upon His Eternal
Humanity that our eternal life depends^p." He, the Second
Adam, will ever remain the Head of the new creation.
The Head implies dominion as well as union; and "of
His kingdom there shall be no end." "To him that over-
cometh," He says, "will I grant to sit with Me in My
Throne; even as I also overcame and am set down with
My Father in His Throne." And here we see the distinc-
tion. "If we suffer with Him, we shall also reign with
Him;" enthroned together with Him. "My Throne,"
this is the place and dignity of the Church, the Bride of
Christ; but "My Father's Throne" is the place of Divine
Majesty. To sit at the right hand of God is to have
a God-like royalty, to which no mere creature can attain^q.
The nearest approach that the creature can make to the
Divine essence, is to sit upon His throne with Christ as
Man, Who as God sits on the throne of the Father.

And this may help us somewhat towards finding

ⁿ See St. Chrysostom *in loc.*

^o Theophylact, Comm. in 1 Cor. xv. Ὁρᾷς ὅτι τὸ, ἄχρις, οὐ πρὸς ἀναίρεσιν τοῦ, μετὰ ταῦτα, κεῖται· ἀλλὰ δι᾽ ἣν εἴρηται αἰτίαν. κρατεῖ γὰρ, φησὶν, αὐτοῦ ἡ βασιλεία, καὶ οὐκ ἀτονεῖ ἕως οὗ πάντα κατορθώσει· μεθ᾽ ὃ δὲ κατορθώσει, πολλῷ μᾶλλον· τῆς γὰρ βασιλείας αὐτοῦ οὐκ ἔσται τέλος.

^p "Our corruptible bodies could never live the life they shall live, were it not that here they are joined with His Body which is incorruptible, and that His is in our's as a cause of immortality, a cause by removing, through the death and merit of His own flesh, that which hindered the life of our's."
—*Hooker*, bk. v. § 56.   ^q See J. Mede, Works, p. 905.

a meaning for the last words of the text, which assign the object and the result of this delivering up of the Kingdom, namely, "that God may be all in all."

At present we can only approach to God through the Mediator, Who is both God and Man. He is now the "living way" to the Father. First the Church is drawn up into Himself and purified; and then, at length, joined through Him to God, "that God may be all in all." But when the purified Church shall have been placed upon the Throne of Christ, then shall the saints approach directly to God, as nearly, at least, as the finite can approach to the Infinite. This intimate communion with God—the Father, the Son, and the Holy Ghost—is the last and highest of the creature's aspirations. Then shall we see face to face, and know even as we are known. So that the delivering up of the Kingdom is the bringing of the saints into the very Presence-chamber of God. It is the removal of the last barrier—the taking away of all that is intermediate—the unfolding of the doors which shall reveal to our sight the King in His beauty, the infinite rest and everlasting portion of the soul.

Brethren, I have thus spoken to you of the termination of the mighty struggle with evil, and of the delivering up of the Kingdom. Let us not fail to remember that it is a struggle in which each one of us is now taking part, and that in any case it must end in our subjection to God. The only question is, whether that subjection shall be the voluntary obedience of the son, or the constrained submission of the slave. And this question must be answered NOW. Each day, as it passes, is moulding us for eternity. The question therefore is, What am I now? Am I now yielding myself up to God, or am I resisting the call of His Spirit? There is no neutral position. "He that is not with Me," says Christ, "is against Me." Whatever, then, the secret verdict of your conscience may be, fall down before His Throne, where He yet sits as Mediator, and tell Him that you are resolved to be, henceforth, wholly His. The end cometh, when He will sit as Mediator no longer. The delivering up of the Kingdom closes the time of mercy and intercession. Come to Him then, now, as your Saviour, before you are called to meet Him as your Judge.

So shall you stand at His right hand in that dread day, and enter into the visible unity of His Eternal Kingdom.

www.ingramcontent.com/pod-product-compliance
Lightning Source LLC
Chambersburg PA
CBHW021838230426
43669CB00008B/1006